Warm and joyful stories from childhood

The Funny Things Kids Say

Will Brighten Any Day

Grace Witwer Housholder

*With Watercolors
by Debbie Rittenhouse*

Volume II

This book
belongs to _____

The Funny Things Kids Say Will Brighten Any Day
Volume 2

Published by Vanatech Press

Text © 1995 by Grace Witwer Housholder
Illustrations © 1995 by Debbie Rittenhouse

All rights reserved. No part of this book shall be reproduced, stored in a retrieval system or transmitted by any means, electronic, mechanical, photocopying, recording, or otherwise, without written permission from the author and illustrator. While every precaution has been taken in the preparation of this book, the publisher and authors assume no responsibility for errors or omissions. For more information, write to:

Grace Witwer Housholder
816 Mott Street
Kendallville, IN 46755

If you need more copies of this book and cannot find it in a local store, call Grace Witwer Housholder at 219-347-0738.

Library of Congress Catalog Card Number: 94-061100

Publisher's Cataloging in Publication
(Prepared by Quality Books Inc.)

Housholder, Grace Witwer.
　　The funny things kids say will brighten any day. Vol. II / Grace Witwer Housholder ; with watercolors by Debbie Rittenhouse.
　　p. cm.
　　ISBN 0-9638715-5-2(hardcover)
　　ISBN 0-9638715-6-0(softcover)

　　1. Children--Quotations.　I. Rittenhouse, Debbie, ill.　II. Title.

PN6328.C5H68 1995　　　　　　081'.083
　　　　　　　　　　　　　　　QBI95-20483

10 9 8 7 6 5 4 3 2 1
Printed in the United States of America
First Printing October 1995

Foreword

We are a society that highly values, even glorifies, action. Our toddlers play with action heroes like the Power Rangers, transforming the tiny plastic figures into a multi-million dollar business. Teenagers and adults, alike, rush to see action movies that have made superstars of actors such as Sylvester Stallone and Arnold Schwarzenaegger. "Actions speak louder than words," we are told. "Just do it!" we are encouraged. Everywhere the emphasis is on action.

Yet, it is language that truly empowers the human race, giving it the capacity to formulate, to understand and to communicate complex thoughts and ideas. Without communication through language there could be little or no science, art, literature, philosophy, government or commerce, the hallmarks of what we consider civilization. There would be little or no cooperation among persons or groups, and little or no advancement. Language is the essential tool that enables human beings to understand one another and to manipulate the world around them.

From an infant's earliest exposure to language as the proud parents "ooh" and "aaah" over their new arrival, to the long, intense exchanges between parent and teenager as the boundaries of childhood are being outgrown and the threshhold of adulthood is broached, communication — talking and listening to one another — is vital to a child's growth and development.

Conversations with our children teach them much more than the mechanics of the English language. By talking to our children about the world around them and by answering their questions, we pass on our culture. By taking time to listen to what they have to say we help shape their self-concept, enabling them to see themselves as worthwhile individuals capable of making a positive contribution to the world of which they are a part. By sharing our feelings with them and telling them of past experiences and lessons we have learned, we help to mold their world view and to shape their values.

Language — that powerful tool of civilization and progress — can also be devastatingly destructive to the growth and development of a child. Used as a weapon to hurt and to wound, language can cripple, stunt or distort the blossoming individual. The repeated use of unflattering labels can result in self-fulfilling prophecies. The child who is constantly called "stupid" will act stupid because he believes he is stupid. And the child whose questions go unanswered, whose comments and observations are consistently ignored, will feel unworthy of attention.

How intensely our children hunger for positive communication with us, their parents, is illustrated by Dr. John Trent, co-author of the book, "Leaving The Light On." He tells of a father who scheduled a "date" with his young daughter with the specific purpose of "affirming" or encouraging her with positive words. He took her to a local fast-food restaurant for breakfast and sitting across from her, giving her his complete attention, he said, "Jenny, I want you to know how much I love you and how special you are to Mom and me." He continued, "You're growing up to be a wonderful girl, and we couldn't be more proud of you."

Having said that, he picked up his fork to continue his breakfast when a tiny hand reached over to stop him and a pleading voice said, "Longer, Daddy, longer." So precious were those words to Jenny that she didn't want them to stop!

Whether precious or pugnacious, our words to our children will help determine the adults they become. Of equal importance, though, is the attention we give to their words, their thoughts, their questions. By valuing what they have to say, by truly listening to them, we demonstrate to them their worth as individuals.

It is true that words without the appropriate actions can be hollow and insincere, but there is real power in communicating with our children. As our words teach and direct, encourage and affirm, and as we listen to and record, and value and appreciate their words to us, we are conveying by language and by action those powerful words, "I love you."

Cindy Griebel

(Cindy Griebel is the mother of two daughters. She has a bachelor's degree in education and more than 10 years of experience in early childhood education. She writes a newspaper column called "Positive Parenting." Her husband, the Rev. Paul Griebel, is pastor of St. John Lutheran Church, Kendallville, Ind.)

Table of Contents

Foreward, iii
About the people who created this book, ix
The miracle of organ donation, x
Chapter One Little Angels, 13
Chapter Two Great-Grandmother Grace's Stories, 27
Chapter Three Spoonerisms, Malapropisms and Word Play, 33
Chapter Four Serving Up Smiles, 39
Chapter Five Kids At Work, 45
Chapter Six Kids At Play, 49
Chapter Seven The Most Important Thing Is Her Smile, 53
Chapter Eight That's My Boy! 55
Chapter Nine The World According To Kids, 61
Chapter Ten And The Band Played On, 69
Chapter Eleven Bathroom Humor, 75
Chapter Twelve Dressing For Success, 83
Chapter Thirteen Kids and the Birds and the Bees, 85
Chapter Fourteen Kids and Marriage, 93
Chapter Fifteen Teaching About Money Takes All the Cents You Have, 99
Chapter Sixteen There's No Such Thing As A Foolish Question, 101
Chapter Seventeen When Mum's The Word For An Aspiring Singer, 105
Chapter Eighteen Potpourri, 107
Chapter Nineteen The First Day of School, 113
Chapter Twenty Two Boys and a Picture, 115
Chapter Twenty-One To Grandparents' House We Go, 119
Chapter Twenty-Two Little Elves (Christmas Stories), 125
Chapter Twenty-Three A Homemaker Is Priceless, 131
Our Family Stories 139

Table of Illustrations

"Train up a child in the way he should go: and when he is old, he will not depart from it." (Proverbs 22:6) vii

"Jesus collects balloons to give to people when they enter heaven." 15

"Let them praise his name with dancing." (Psalm 149:3) 17

"Oh! There's a ground chuck!" 23

"Take it! It's leaking!" 25

"I'm going on a fish hunt!" 31

"Do you know what this is? It's a subway, but not the kind you can eat!" 65

"Here's the police! Everyone put their seatbelts on!" 71

"Wow, that guy had on strong aftershave lotion! I could smell it clear through the phone!" 73

"What's chipping away his head?" 79

Told his batting average was going down, Chuck said, "Yes, my batteries are running down!" 81

Mrs. Becker said the kittens get their milk from the bumps on Midnight's tummy. "Does she have Pepsi ones, too?" 87

"No gravy today. I want naked potatoes!" 89

"Do you take this man to be your awful-headed husband?" 95

"I'm NOT sitting on your lap! If you give me your phone number, I'll call you when I have time!" 129

"A chicken that lays eggs is a ___ (hen). One boy wrote 'MOM.'" 135

"OK, Daddy. I ready go for ride!" 137

The children were told to cross their legs and sit like pretzels... "But I like straight pretzels!" 143

"I didn't think I'd have anything like this until my WEDDING!" 145

Noah the cat is 98 in cat years. "Does Noah know he is an adult?" 151

"Train up a child in the way he should go: and when he is old, he will not depart from it." (Proverbs 22:6)

About the people who created this book...

Grace Witwer Housholder started her column "The Funny Things Kids Say Will Brighten Any Day" in The (Kendallville, Ind.) News-Sun in 1987. This is her second "Funny Kids" book.

An award-winning journalist, Grace holds journalism and French degrees from Indiana University. She and her husband, Terry, the managing editor of The News-Sun, have four children: Dorothy (Dolly), 16; Elizabeth, 13; Catherine, 10; and Paul, 8. They are active in the community and at Immanuel Lutheran Church, Avilla.

Debbie Rittenhouse, who holds a fine arts degree from Bowling Green State University, is widely acclaimed for her watercolors. She and her husband Jerry, the pastor of Harvest Community Church in Kendallville, have four children: Katie, 12; Ben, 10; Luke, 7; and Seth, 3. Debbie uses her artistic and musical talents to benefit her church and her community.

With their publishing skills, Susan and Fred Klopfer of Vanatech Press have helped the "Funny Kids" books to take shape. Special thanks go to the Klopfers; to Jon Davis, Jim Werner and Mary Bender at The News-Sun, who helped with the cover, pictures and layout; to Nick Smith, Karen Shultz, Janet Deahl and Courier Corporation, Kendallville; to Cindy Griebel for writing the foreward; to Debra Hockley and Carol Ernsberger for proofreading; and to my husband, Terry, for his assistance.

But the biggest thank you goes to News-Sun readers who have shared their funny stories.

Because so much of this book is based on stories from the community, we are giving a major portion of any profit from this book to the Cole Center Family YMCA, a Noble County organization that enriches the lives of children and their families in many ways.

Do you have a funny story?

When a child says something that makes you laugh, the first thing you should do is write it down on any piece of scrap paper that is handy. Then as soon as possible transfer the story to the blank pages at the end of this book. You will slowly but steadily acquire a one-of-a-kind collection of humorous, happy memories!

If you would like to see your story in print, please send it to Grace Witwer Housholder, 816 Mott St., Kendallville, IN 46755. (If you enclose a stamped, self-addressed envelope, Grace will send you a copy of the "Funny Kids" column in which your story appears.)

Thank you in advance for sharing your stories. It's people like you who make the "Funny Kids" books possible.

You are holding in your hands evidence of a miracle.

Had it not been for the miracle of organ donation Debbie Rittenhouse, the illustrator of this book, would be blind.

Every time Debbie picks up a brush to paint, she silently thanks God for the talent he gave her.

Then she offers another prayer — a fervant thank you for the gift of sight.

Debbie underwent a painful and very risky cornea transplant during the winter of 1994. She has Terrians Degenerative Syndrome which makes her corneas "melt" away.

When the severity of her cornea problem was discovered, she was put at the top of the nation's transplant list. Within two weeks, she was on the operating table at St. Vincent's Hospital in Indianapolis. Dr. Frances Price used two perfect corneas to make sure that he had enough to create the crescent shape.

"I'd love to be able to tell the family of the donor what a gift that was," she says. All Debbie knows is that the corneas came from a 78-year-old person from Missouri.

"Until you are on a waiting list, you don't take transplants that seriously," she adds.

There are no guarantees that the problem won't reoccur. In fact, just after Debbie completed painting the pictures for this book, she learned that she would have to have a cornea transplant in her other eye.

"It's a little bit scary," Debbie says. "But I trust that God will take care of me. He has already worked a miracle in my left eye."

Debbie knows that sight is a gift from God, and that as long as God wants her to paint, he will supply her with the gift of sight.

***

If you have not yet done so, please talk about organ and tissue donation with your family. Physicians and hospital personnel can answer your questions and/or give you brochures with information about organ and tissue donation.

It is important that family members know your wishes, because they are the ones who will be asked to make the decision.

*This book is dedicated to my four children
and to children everywhere
who make people smile.*

Chapter One

Little Angels

If there is anything more comforting than holding a child close to you and rocking, it is probably having a child seek out your hand and grasp it tightly. The feel of a child's warm body, bursting with love, energy and young life, gives hope and comfort to adults who are tired and discouraged.

The pure and simple faith of children is inspirational. Jesus said, "Let the children come to me, for the Kingdom of God belongs to such as they." (Mark 10:14) Maybe that's why we often call children "Little Angels."

On her fifth birthday, Amanda wanted all her friends and relatives supplied with helium balloons. Even though the adults had heard such balloons are sometimes dangerous to wildlife, they followed Amanda's instructions to let them go.

"Jesus collects them so that he has one to give each person when they enter heaven," Amanda explained.

When Mrs. Cox's grandsons saw mountains out West for the first time, they looked at their height in amazement. The mountains seemed to extend into the sky.

"When we get there we'll walk right up to the top and say, 'Hello, Jesus!'" the boys said.

The teacher of the Sunday school class for 5-year-olds learned that the father of one of her students doesn't go to church.

"Let's pray that he starts coming to church," the teacher told the class.

"It's gonna take more than that!" the daughter said.

Dustin, 5, told his mother, "I wish God would have given me a parachute to come down from heaven with."

Jarrod, Evy, Seagan and Nick went trick-or-treating at Dr. Warrener's home. As the doctor's son handed out treats, the father of the four children told them that the boy handing out treats was the son of the man who brought all four of them into the world.

"What!" Jarrod, 5, exclaimed. "HE'S JESUS!"

Chapter One

Paul, 7, was walking with Terry and me past the Immaculate Conception Catholic Church. Terry and I commented on how nice the church's new addition looks.

"When they remodel a church, does the pastor pay for it?" Paul asked.

One night Debra read the Bible story about the prodigal son to Mark. Mark had many questions, and Debra tried to answer them.

When Mark's father came to tuck Mark in, Debra asked Mark to tell his father the main idea of the story.

Mark thought and thought. And then his face lit up. "I know — never take your share 'til your father's dead!"

Mrs. Griebel was singing "He's Got the Whole World in His Hands" with the preschool children. She told the children that God has sisters, brothers, parents, grandparents, aunts, uncles, etc. in his hands.

Lacey looked at her hands and said, "His hands are a whole lot bigger than mine!"

The class was talking about God's rules that help and protect us. The class was listing the rules on a big sheet of paper. Here's one from Adam that you might not have heard: "Don't put bananas in the recycling center!"

The Ogles drove by a gravel pit. There was a lake beside the pit.

"How deep can they make the lake?" Ryan asked.

They talked about how the company can keep digging and digging.

"They can keep digging until the devil comes out!" said Andrew, 7.

The Kids' Choir of Harvest Community Church traveled to sing in a local nursing home. Before they left for the new experience, the choir members joined in prayer.

The song leader overheard Korey, 9, say the following prayer: "Dear God, please don't let any of the people in the nursing home die before we get there!"

When Katie and Ben were quite young, they were talking about what heaven would be like.

Ben said the lights in heaven would be on all the time.

"There aren't any lights in heaven," Katie said.

"Yes, there are!"

They argued back and forth, but Ben had the last word: "Yes, there are — the Israelites!"

"Jesus collects balloons to give to people when they enter heaven."

"Let them praise his name with dancing." (Psalm 149:3)

Funny Kids

Frankie, 4, asked if he and his brother Wilson, 3, could have a Flintstones vitamin. Brenda, who was in another room, said yes. Then she heard Frankie lead Wilson in the following prayer: "Jesus, thank you for the vitamin and the sun and the clouds and the rain!"

After a pause Frankie said to Wilson, "You may be seated and eat it!"

Kenny, 4, drove past a cemetery. "You have to be dead to live there," he said.

When Kenny's grandfather was buried, Kenny asked if the people buried around his grandpa were neighbors.

Several weeks later when they visited the cemetery Kenny noticed some new graves. "I see Grandpa has some new neighbors," he said.

Kenny and Laura were coloring Easter eggs. Kenny said he was going to make an egg for Grandpa.

Laura said, "You can't make an egg for Grandpa 'cause he died, Kenny."

"Yes, I can."

"Well, how are you going to give it to him?"

Kenny thought for a while and said, "I'll mail it to God."

Vi, an attorney, does some of her work at home. One day she was consulting a huge book about taxes.

Chuck, 3, discovered his mother studying the big tax book.

"What kind of Bible is that?" he asked.

Catherine, 4, said she wanted to reach up and touch the clouds. Carmen, her mother, told her that she can't touch them because they are too high.

"Then I need to buy WINGS!" Catherine said.

Mrs. Buuck asked the kindergarten students what Isaac's twin sons were named.

Peter, 5, raised his hand and said, "Seesaw?"

David, 2, was listening to the story of David and Goliath for the first time. When he heard that David hit Goliath with a stone and killed him, he said, "I won! I won!"

Chapter One

Ron was saying his prayers: "Dear God, bless everyone the whole world through. And please help everyone to do whatever I want them to. Amen."

Terry sternly ordered the four children to pick up the toys that were strewn throughout the entire downstairs.
Paul, 5, just stood there.
"Get to work!" Terry said sternly.
Paul looked at Terry defiantly and said, "You're not the boss!"
"I'm not?" Terry said with anger and surprise. "Well, who is?"
"Jesus!" Paul yelled triumphantly.

Jill, 6, was used to seeing a certain gentleman in church always doze off. One Sunday when all the members of the congregation bowed their heads for silent prayer, Jill whispered loudly, "Mom, look! EVERYBODY'S sleeping!"

Catherine, 8, reported that her Sunday school teacher told the class they were going to talk about kings, and then asked the students to name some kings.
"Elvis!" one student replied.

Vi found Chuck, 3, at the bathroom sink. He had been playing, and he was very wet, especially his head.
"What are you doing?" she asked.
Vi could see by his expression that the wheels in his mind were turning double-time as he tried to come up with an acceptable explanation.
In a few seconds he settled on what to tell her. "I'm baptizing myself!" he said.

During the children's sermon, the children were asked what makes them scared.
Tara piped up, "I get scared when my mom makes popcorn because the smoke alarm goes off!"

A little girl was driving with her grandmother when she noticed several tall radio towers. She asked what they were, and her grandmother explained.
After a while the little girl said thoughtfully, "I bet those towers tickle Jehovah's belly!"

Kyrie', 3, was saying her prayers with her grandmother, Olga. At the end of her prayer, she had one more request for God: Could she go to Chuck E Cheese?
Then Olga said her prayer, concluding with "Amen."
"You can't say 'amen,'" Kyrie' told Olga. "You haven't told God that you're taking me to Chuck E Cheese!"

Funny Kids

On a rainy day Elizabeth, 5, drove with her brother, Max, past a cemetery. They saw preparations for a burial with a large canopy.

"Look, Mom, someone is CAMPING in that cemetery!" Elizabeth exclaimed.

After work Pam picks up her daughters, Heather and Hilary, and drives them home. Invariably, the two girls start bickering.

"Every afternoon when I pick you up, I pray that you won't argue in the car," Pam wearily told the girls one day.

"Well, keep on praying," Heather said.

Kristen, 9, and Staci, 8, were having an argument in the back seat of the car. Staci's mom, Janet, was carefully watching them in the rearview mirror. She saw Staci reach over and pinch Kristen. Kristen then hit Staci, causing her to yell, "Mom... Kristen hit me!"

"But you started it," Janet said.

"I did not!"

"I don't think you're telling the truth."

"Fine," Staci replied. "When you die, ask God!"

Kristen was talking about the new Hispanic girl in their fourth-grade class. One child said, "You're prejudiced."

"I am not," Kristen replied indignantly. "I'm Catholic!"

At a confirmation dinner a little girl came up to Laura, Pastor Bearman's wife, and pointed to Pastor Bearman.

"Does Jesus like poppyseed rolls?" the little girl whispered to Laura.

A priest was showing some very young Vacation Bible School students what was behind different doors in their church. In one closet he keeps the monstrance, which is used to display Holy Communion.

That night at supper, while talking about Vacation Bible School, one of the children that had been on the priest's tour announced, "Father has a mistress in the closet!"

Jeff, 3, told Chuck, 6, that he was never going to sin again.

Chuck told him that it isn't possible to stop sinning, because everybody sins.

"But my sins will be good sins," Jeff said.

Chapter One

Jason was walking along the road with his mother when they saw a snake.
"Stay away from that snake!" Karla said.
"What will the snake do to me, Mom?"
"Just scare the devil out of you, that's all."
After thinking for a little while, Jason said, "Good. Now I have the devil out of me and only Jesus left in me!"

The Herricks live on a street that has a lot of EMS traffic. Sue tried to teach the boys to say a prayer for the patients, medical workers and drivers whenever they hear the siren. After a particularly busy day for the EMS, there was yet another siren.
Matt, who was always good about saying his prayers, rolled his eyes and said, "Here we go again, God!"

Erin, a first-grade student at St. John Lutheran School, was going over the Bible verse that she was supposed to learn for the week. Out of the blue she told her mother, Hayley, "I know the Ten Commandments!"
"You do?" Hayley said. "Let's hear them."
This is what Erin carefully told her mother:
1. Don't praise false gods.
2. Don't kill.
3. Jesus should be the only important thing in our hearts.
4. Don't push.
5. Be nice to your friends.
6. Don't let your eyeballs roll on someone else's paper. (Don't cheat.)
7. Obey your parents.
8. Don't steal.
9. Don't take drugs.
10. Follow the recipe!

"Oh! There's a ground chuck!"

"Take it! It's leaking!"

Chapter Two

Great-Grandmother Grace's Stories

Through the generations it has been the custom in our family to name children after their parents, grandparents, aunts or uncles. Sometimes it gets confusing, but that's the way we do it. My father was named after his grandfather. My mother was named after her mother. I was named after my great-grandmother, Grace Woodard Osburn.

**Grace Osburn
of Owosso, Mich.**

Great-Grandmother Grace cradled me in her arms. But I never got to know her because she died when I was 6 months old.

My father adored Great-Grandmother Grace (he and Aunt Vi called her Gaga) and she doted on her grandchildren. For many years she only had two: dad (who everyone called Corky) and Violette, who was six years younger.

Dad remembers that Great-Grandmother Grace was beautiful, stylish, artistic and witty. She had been the most beautiful girl in Michigan, he was told.

Great-Grandmother Grace loved telling funny stories. One of her favorites was about the time her neighbor lady in Owosso phoned from across the street. After a lengthy conversation, when she was just about to hang up, the lady remembered the point of her call.

"Oh, by the way, Mrs. Osburn," the lady said, "Did you know your little boy is hanging out the third floor window?!"

Chapter Two

Great-Grandmother Grace's house was around the corner from the childhood home of Thomas E. Dewey, the Republican candidate for president in 1944 and 1948. Dad remembers in 1944 being pushed in his soap box derby car by his friend Sonny as they led a parade down Oliver Street to the Dewey homestead where Dewey was going to make a campaign speech. Before the speech people stood awkwardly on Annie Dewey's front porch while a photographer tried to arrange them around the local hero. People were quiet and no one knew what to say. While the photographer was moving people here and there, Great-Grandmother Grace broke the silence with the question: "Do we (Dewey) look OK?!"

Shortly after my first "Funny Kids" book came out, Aunt Vi called to tell me about a small leather book she had discovered in a desk in my Grandmother Witwer's house. It was Great-Grandmother Grace's collection of funny stories about Dad and Aunt Vi... a book I don't think anyone knew existed. The book has about 70 stories covering a 10-year span before World War II.

When I started collecting funny stories in 1987, little did I know I was following in my great-grandmother's footsteps!

The following stories are copied almost word for word from Great-Grandmother Grace's neat handwriting. Most of the stories are from when Dad was 4 or 5 years old.

We were all downstairs in the living room, and Corky had gone to bed. We heard his little feet pattering about. Mohler (Corky's father) went up and scolded him for getting out of bed.

"Why you wouldn't get out of bed like this even when you were a little baby," Mohler said.

"Why of course not," Corky said. "I couldn't walk then!"

On our trip to California Corky was good as gold. When we got to Lordsburg he said, "I s'pose when people get to Lordsburg they say, 'Oh Lord, here we are in Lordsburg.'"

28

Funny Kids

He is never given candy. One day after he had eaten a particularly good meal, I gave him a large marshmallow covered with chocolate. It almost overcame him to be given such a thing out of a clear sky, and he said, "We're not so darn 'fraid of a little piece of candy, are we Gaga?"

Jane (Corky's mother) told him not to put any more water in the radiator, but he kept on until it ran over. She said if he had listened to her it wouldn't have run over.

"I know you are more intelligent and older and more clever and have had more experience," he told Jane. "But I know a good many things that you have forgotten!"

One day I heard Corky cry in the kitchen. He said, "Ah-wa (Hulda, the maid) put soap in my mouth."

She said Corky said "gosh" so she washed out his mouth. I told her I had heard her say it and if she said it again Corky could put soap in her mouth. I also told her not to put soap in his mouth again. That very afternoon Corky played on the floor in the porch. Hulda slipped. He jumped right up and ran for the soap, and she had her mouth washed...

(A few days later) I was hurrying to put up the kitchen curtains. Corky said, "Gaga, you take me for my nap and not Ah-wa."

I said, "I would like to get these curtains up before your mama comes, so let Hulda take you."

He slapped his hand against his leg and said, "Oh gosh!"

Then realizing he had said something bad, he looked at Hulda and said, "I mean, Oh! Hell!"

When Violette, Corky's sister was born, he went to his mama and said "Mom, can't you get a little boy right now?" Later he asked, "Am I its uncle?"

Violette, little precious, had an earache. She was so good and patient, but restless. "Gaga," she said. "See what's the matter with me. Maybe if I could blow up (throw up) I'd feel better!"

Once Violette, age 3, wet the bed. The little darling never does. "I didn't wet the bed, Gaga," she said. "I sweat."

Corky was saying his prayer, "Love is an angel shining fair..." He got stuck in the middle and said in the same tone, "For unto us a child is born."

"I'm going on a fish hunt!"

Chapter Three
Spoonerisms, Malapropisms and Word Play

Many of the funny things kids say are based on spoonerisms ("patterkiller" for caterpillar), unintentional plays on words ("body shop" for funeral home) or metaphors, like the boy zipped into a sleeping bag who said, with obvious satisfaction, "It feels like a hot dog bun." But by far the largest category of kid-creations is the malapropism. Mrs. Malaprop, the busybody in Richard Sheridan's 1775 play, "The Rivals," went around saying things like, "He is the very pineapple of politeness." Our children do the same, sometimes making us laugh out loud, sometimes opening our eyes to new perceptions.

Dina, 3, stepped on a bumble bee. Her mother quickly came to the rescue and pulled out the stinger.
"You'll be OK now, honey," Mrs. Bange said. "Mama got the bee."
"I know, Mama," Dina said. "But the bumble still hurts!"

Catherine, 7, was telling her friends about attending the Gymnastics Spectacular in Indianapolis. She said that her parents (Terry and I who are reporters) got to sit really close to the gymnasts because they had "trespasses" (press passes)!

Lindsey, 4, was asked to name the days of the week. She said, "Monday, Tuesday, Wednesday, Thursday, Friday and yesterday!"

The first time she saw a convertible, Charissa excitedly shouted, "Mommy, there's a car with no lid!"

Ann, visiting her grandparents, startled the assembled family by announcing, "It's raining like hail out there!"

Chad said he will go on a "fish hunt" someday.

Chapter Three

Ben, 4, was looking up at the sky at some seagulls. "Look, Mom, it's the American seagull," he said.

Driving home from Fort Wayne, LaRea noticed a ground hog. She pointed it out to her little sister, Niccole. A little while later LaRea saw a woodchuck, which she also pointed out to Niccole.
Niccole started eagerly looking for nature on her own. After a few minutes, she called out, "Oh, there's a ground chuck!"

Mrs. Griebel took her preschool class on a trip to Dr. Barnard's veterinary clinic. They saw a lot of different animals. For days the children talked about visiting "Dr. Barnyard!"

Telling about his visit to "Dr. Barnyard's," Paul said with excitement, "We saw horses and baby horses and dogs and puppy dogs and EVEN cat puppies (kittens)!"

Janet was tickling Staci, 5. Hearing the commotion, Kristen, 7, called from the other room, "What are you doing out there?"
Staci replied, "None of your..." And then she stopped to think of the right word. "Earwax!" She had been trying to think of beeswax.

Drew, 3, heard his stomach growl.
"Oh, Jody," Drew said. "Did you hear my stomach sing?"

Jeanna, 2, looked up into the night sky and pointed at the crescent moon.
"Look at that big banana in the sky!" she exclaimed.

Alecia, 4, told her teacher about the night her dog was fighting. Her father went outside with a flashlight to see what was going on, and it was "A HIPPOPOSSUM!"

Alecia went fishing. As she waited for a bite, she called to all the fish in the lake, "Here fishy, fishy! Come and get your lunch!"
When she went home, she proudly announced that she had caught some "blue girls!"

We were talking about the twins we know when Catherine, 7, decided to broaden the subject.
"Do you know any triplets?" she asked.
We said no, not personally.
"Do you know any four-flips?" she asked.

Funny Kids

One of Mrs. Griebel's preschoolers referred to the swing set as the sling shot.

A 10-year-old was playing at our house when she bent back her baby finger. "My finger's broken," she wailed. "I know it's broken!"
I told her I didn't think it was broken.
"Will I have to have surgery?" she asked, tears rolling down her cheeks.
"Of course not," I said.
"Oh, good," she said, starting to calm down. "I always think things are worse than they are. My mom says I'm hypodermic!" She meant to stay hypochondriac.

While in the hospital Meghann asked her mother what nurses do. Janet said they help doctors with things like surgery. She explained that surgery is when you have operations like taking out your tonsils, appendix, gall bladder, etc.
"Yeah, and butterflies," Meghann said.
"Butterflies?" Janet asked.
"You know, butterflies in your stomach!"

Catherine, 9, wanted some time to herself, but Paul, 7, wouldn't leave her alone. Catherine repeatedly told Paul to go away, but he stuck to her like glue.
Catherine came into the kitchen with Paul hanging on her back. "Mom, Paul's addicted to me!" she said.

When Jenni asks Max, 1, how a cow goes, Max says, "Moo!" A duck? "Quack, quack." A cat? "Meow!" A dog? "Woof, woof!"
When asked how Mommy goes, he shakes his head, points a finger and replies, "No! No!"

Sarah, 3, likes to wear dresses. But sometimes her mother prefers pants outfits for her. One day, over Sarah's protestations, Nancy put a cute pants outfit on Sarah and told her she looked marvelous.
"I do not!" Sarah said.
"Do you know what marvelous means?" her mother asked.
"It means you've lost your marbles," Sarah sniffed.

Kimberly, 7, was playing with friends with the Nintendo. When her friend Gregg lost he said, "I got screwed."
"You can't get screwed," Kimberly said. "You don't have screws in you."

Chapter Three

Asked the name of her preschool teacher, Samantha thought for a minute and said "Mrs. Money."

The teacher was Mrs. Nichols.

Paul, 5, called to a cat that was in our backyard. The cat looked at Paul and ran away.

"That's a scaredy-cat," Paul said.

Aaron told his mother that he couldn't walk any farther because his feet were "out of breath!"

At a basketball game, Jamison was looking across the gym at the opposing bleachers, trying to find his grandparents.

"It's like a 'Where's Waldo' book, isn't it?" he told his mom.

When Rebecca, 5, saw her teen-age cousin without her retainer in her mouth, she asked, "Where's your teeth holder?"

Jeff, 2, asked his mother, "When am I going to have a lost tooth?"

Emily saw the specially made toddler beds that were used by 3-year-old twins Jalyn and Jalyssa.

Emily later told her brother Brock about the twins' little beds. "You should see their beds," she said. "They're DWARF beds!"

Peering at a crescent-shaped moon, Aaron said the moon was melting. On a very hot day he said he thought the sun was boiling.

One day Paul mixed all sorts of things like mustard, catsup, sugar, water and celery leaves to see what would happen. It was a disgusting combination, and I wanted to throw it away. Just as I was about to pour it down the garbage disposal, Paul caught sight of me and yelled, "Mom! Don't sink it!"

Susan found a green horn worm and showed it to Zane. He told her that it was a John Deere worm.

Rebecca, 4, told her grandma, "I feel like I have a tornado in my stomach!"

Funny Kids

A kindergarten student named Antonia couldn't remember Miss Marshall's name so she called her "TEE-cher."

Andy, the student sitting next to Antonia, asked Miss Marshall one day, "Why does she call you a T-shirt?"

I told our children they better pack light for vacation.
"Mom, I can't pack light. I always pack heavy," Liz said.
"I thought you meant pack a flashlight!" Catherine, 8, said with surprise.

Lucy, 10, told her mother that her 4-H group made $190.20 selling concussions (concessions).

Deidre told her mother, "I don't want to go tomorrow. I want to go to now!" (Right now)

Dani, 7, was all excited when her sister came home from having her eyes tested for school.
Running out to meet her, Dani asked, "Well, did you have any cavities?"

Zane, 4, told his mother that he saw a bee. When she asked him where it was, he said, "It is beeing around me!"

One day Debbie took her son Luke into the women's restroom at the mall. He washed his hands and used the blow dryer. Later he told his father, "They had this thing to dry your hands. It was automagic!"

Rebecca, 5, may become the first female head of the CIA. This is how she recited the Pledge of Allegiance to her parents: ..."and to the Republic for which it stands, one nation, UNDERCOVER, with liberty and justice for all."

Jon, 3, told his grandmother, "I REALLY NEED a Tic-Tac!"
"Why do you need a Tic-Tac?" she asked.
"My breath hurts!"

Chris's kindergarten teacher was holding her throat because she had laryngitis. She told the children that she had a frog in her throat.
"Hold your neck tighter," Chris said. "Maybe the frog will jump out!"

Miss Howard was telling her first-grade students about hurricanes, tornadoes and other kinds of weather.
Troy raised his hand and said, "And we can have earth shakes, too!"

Chapter Three

When Bambi saw a stroller with triplets, she told her grandfather, Gabby, "Granddad, look! She's got three twins!"

Ben, 9, was ordering Luke around. With his hands on his hips, Luke said angrily, "I'm not your serpent!"

Lucy was on a long car trip with Isabella, 2. Isabella threw up — something she had never done before.
Lucy pulled off the highway so that she could help Isabella. Looking at her mother with her huge eyes, Isabella said, "I'm sorry, Mommy. I spilled."

Matt was making a terrible face while eating a Popsicle. Asked what the matter was, he said, "The Popsicle makes my teeth shiver."

Brett took his daughters Kaitlin and Emily to the grocery store. They parked next to any Amish buggy.
"Dad, what do you call those people again?" asked Kaitlin, 7.
"They're Amish."
Kaitlin was quiet for several seconds, obviously thinking very hard.
"Dad, do you call their babies omelettes?" she asked.

Aaron, 3, was eating in a restaurant with his mother.
"Can I bring you anything else, ma'am?" the waitress asked.
"Mom, your name isn't ma'am. It's Carla!" Aaron said.

Mrs. Grubb asked the children what they had seen on the ground that morning.
"Frosting!" a student said.

Chuck, 5, was proud that he could put his shoes on the right feet.
"Come and watch me put on my shoes," he said. "I know my right foot from my wrong foot!"

Phyllis' young granddaughter put a table knife in her mouth.
"Whatever are you doing with that in your mouth?" Phyllis asked.
"Cutting teeth," she answered matter-of-factly.

Award-winning author, poet and educator Philip Appleman, who grew up in Kendallville, helped me with the introduction to this chapter and gave me this story for my collection. At age 5, he saw a buggy without a horse nearby and declared, "That buggy hasn't grown a horse yet!"

Chapter Four

Serving Up Smiles

Getting their children to develop good eating habits is often a challenge for parents. With all the television commercials for candy that flies, cereal that talks, beverages that explode and chips that dance, kids are rather disappointed when it's time to eat and their food just sits there!

But no matter what the occasion — a family dinner, a potluck or snack time — take time to listen to the kids. There's a chance you'll hear a comment that will make you grin from ear to ear.

Anita made a pork roast and mashed potatoes for dinner. She was getting ready to put gravy on Matthew's mashed potatoes when he stopped her.

"No gravy today," the 5-year-old said. "I want naked potatoes!"

Jeff, 3, was eating supper when he choked slightly on a piece of food.

"Oops. That must have gone down my breakfast pipe," he told his mother.

Jaime was looking for her son Jason, 4. When she found him, he was unplugging the refrigerator.

She asked him why he was unplugging the refrigerator.

"You know Daddy doesn't like his pop cold," Jason explained.

One rainy afternoon Sue was caring for five children, all under the age of 4. It was snack time so she lined the kids up in front of the china hutch and gave them cups. Then she went to the refrigerator to get out the milk.

She didn't check to see if the lid was on tight. So when she shook the jug, milk shot across the kitchen and splashed onto the carpet in front of the kids.

No one said a word. Finally, Matt looked up at Sue and asked, "Were we supposed to catch it, Sue?"

Kyrie' was eating a watermelon. She told her grandpa that she really likes watermelons, but they are hard to eat because of all the "bones" (seeds)!

Chapter Four

An 11-year-old received some souvenir popcorn that was still on the ear of corn.

She put the ear of corn in the microwave to pop the kernels. Then she called her younger brother. "Come and get some popcorn made just like the Indians used to make it!"

After Thanksgiving vacation a preschool teacher asked her students numerous questions about how their holiday was.

"When I was at Thanksgiving dinner, my teeth began to hurt really bad," Jessi said.

"What happened to make your teeth hurt?"

"I guess I just ate too much dip!"

When Paul Walsdorf was 3, he attended a family dinner at his cousins' house. He was a good eater, and after eating all the dinner and dessert he complimented his aunt about the meal.

"Everything tasted fine," he said, "except for the rust on the pumpkin pie!"

Catherine, 9, wanted to make herself some lunch. She asked where the hot-dogs were and was told to look in the meat drawer of the refrigerator.

"I did," Catherine said. "All there is is 'franks.'"

Rob, a preschooler, was playing with some dishes in the kitchen sink. When LouAnne walked by he handed her a cup of sudsy water and said, "Here, Mom, I made you a cup of 'Al Pacino.'"

Alicia was helping her dad prepare a salad. When he came to the feta cheese, she wondered what it tasted like. He suggested that she try it, and tell him what she thought.

"It tastes just like your throat does right after you throw up," she reported.

A few years ago there was a scare about fruit from Chile being tainted with poison. When Mr. and Mrs. Osterlund heard it on the radio, they agreed that even though they didn't really think there was anything wrong with the fruit in their refrigerator, their children were too precious to even consider placing them in a risky situation.

Holly came down for breakfast just as Mrs. Osterlund said she would throw out the Chilean grapes.

"You can throw out the chili, Mom. But please keep the grapes!" came a little voice from down the hallway.

Funny Kids

Sometimes when Carol serves supper, she puts a variety of food out and everyone serves themselves. When she does that, she calls it smorgasbord.

One time when she announced she was serving dinner smorgasbord style, Karl, 6, moaned, "Oh, no, not drive-up again!"

A grandmother made her grandson a bunny cake with coconut on it. She noticed that he just picked at it, and asked him if he didn't like it.

He said yes, he liked the cake but, "I don't like all this hair in it!"

Austin, 5, came up with all sorts of excuses about why he couldn't finish his baloney sandwich. His mother insisted he had to finish it to get dessert.

Finally, Austin came to Cindy and said, "I can't eat all my bread because there's no baloney left because the baloney slid into my mouth!"

Grandma showed Todd, 7, the chocolate cake she had made from "scratch" especially for him.

Todd looked at the cake with tears in his eyes. "I can't eat any because it might make me itch," he said sorrowfully.

Erika, 3, was eating chips and dip. She buried one of her chips in the dip. "Look, Mom," she said. "I buried one of my chips."

"Why did you do that?"

"Because I want it to grow!"

Carol left a partially-frosted cake in the kitchen to cool.

Karl, 9, came into the kitchen and saw the cake. "Mom," he called, "are you done putting the plaster on the cake?"

Jeri Anne, 4, was making pizza with her grandma. As they put on the toppings, she asked, "Gram, is this a smoking pizza?"

Gram said she didn't understand the question.

Jeri Anne replied, "You know, when we go to Pizza Hut they always ask, 'Smoking or non-smoking?'"

Brody, 6, was in the back seat of the car with some Gummi Bears. He used all 10 fingers to stuff them in his mouth.

"Don't put your fingers in your mouth," his mother, Sue, said. "Your fingers have germs on them."

"But they're MY germs!" Brody mumbled through his mouthful.

Chapter Four

Aaron, 3, awoke on Saturday to the smell of coffeecake in the oven. He asked his mom if it was Sunday. She said it was Saturday.
"But it SMELLS like Sunday," he said.

While Aaron and his father were eating fish sticks one evening, he asked his dad, "How do they get the fish to go inside these fish sticks?"

At lunchtime Grandma fixed baloney sandwiches. When everyone sat down to eat, Jolene asked, "Grandma, what was this when it was real?"
Grandma said she didn't understand the question.
"What was this when it was real? A cow or a pig?" Jolene asked.

It's always a struggle to get Christopher to eat because he is so picky. He was still picking at his food after the rest of the family was done.
His father told him about the starving children in Africa and how happy they would be to sit down to such a nice supper.
Christopher looked at his dad and said, "Why don't we just send them my supper then?"

Three generations of the Maurer family were visiting. Rita complimented the grandmother on the delicious raspberry pie she had made.
Lee, 8, whispered to Rita, "You have to be REAL OLD to cook like that!"

Max, 3, was looking through a book about oceans with his mother. When he saw a picture of a jellyfish, he said, "That's a peanut butter fish!"

When his mother bought crunchy peanut butter instead of smooth, Max complained, "Mom, this peanut butter has seeds in it!"

Karen, 4, refused to eat the lunch that her friend's mother served.
"But you like macaroni and cheese," Karen's mother said.
"It wasn't in the right box," Karen said. (Karen's grandfather was with Kraft Foods for 40 years.)

Mrs. Hunter was talking to her preschool students about Thanksgiving. Haley, 5, announced that her family had had chicken.
Mrs. Hunter was surprised.
After some consideration, Haley said, "Well, maybe that chicken was a turkey!"

Funny Kids

Max's favorite sandwich is a "jelly sandwich with peanut butter but no jelly!"

Jonathan, 3, ate chicken on the bone for the first time. When he got down to the bone in the chicken leg, he said with surprise, "Mom, there's his underwear!"

On their trip to Mexico, Kyrie' asked her grandmother Olga what day it was.
"Thursday," Olga said.
"No, I mean is it chicken day or fish day at Richard's (Restaurant)?" Kyrie' asked, not realizing there was no possibility that they would travel thousands of miles for dinner.

I bought Paul, 5, a candy bar. But he wouldn't share it with me. I pouted.
When he was done he held up two chocolate-covered hands and said, "You can lick my fingers, Mom!"

Erin told her mother that she was excited about going to the Apple Festival to get some "apple critters!" (apple fritters)

On the first day of first grade Brittany's mother forgot to send milk money with her.
Brittany came home and told her mother, "I had to go dry today!"

Katherine, 3, was enjoying a Popsicle when it started dripping.
"Take it!" she told her cousin Heidi. "It's leaking!"

Lillian had prepared Thanksgiving dinner for the family. On the table was a big dish of black olives.
When Debra, 6, spotted the black olives she exclaimed, "Grandma, you burned the olives!"

Amanda, 7, was reading a book to her brother Zane, 2.
"Do you know what this is?" she asked. "It's a subway, but not the kind you can eat!"

Chapter Five

Kids At Work

Author and poet Philip Appleman recalls that when his nephew was asked how his first day of kindergarten went, he replied, "It's just WORK, WORK, WORK!" I guess for children, their work IS going to school or to daycare classes. But work can produce amusing moments, as these stories show.

Amber, a very busy 18-month-old, is in a daycare class with 2-year-olds.

One day one of the 2-year-olds told his mother that he had learned his ABC's. He recited them just the way the teacher had said them in class:

"A, B, C, D, Please sit down Amber, E, F, G, H, I, Amber please sit down, J, K, L, Please sit down Amber..."

On the first day of nursery school a police officer came to give a lesson on safety. When he walked in, everyone was quiet. Samantha turned around and said, "Here's the police. Everyone put their seatbelts on!"

Preschool teacher Mrs. Hunter pointed to the November calendar and said, "Aha! I see something different!" referring to the new shapes on which the numbers for the days of the month had been printed. Mrs. Hunter then asked what the name of the new month was.

All the children responded together, "AHA!"

Kindergarten teacher Mrs. Buuck told the students to bring in things that begin with W, Y or Z.

Chris came up to her and wiggled his loose tooth that was hanging by just a thread of gum. "I brought 'wiggle' for show and tell!" he said.

After settling the children into a new seating arrangement, Mrs. Osterlund noticed a boy with a scowl on his face. It was apparent that he didn't appreciate his new place between two girls.

Noticing the scowl, another boy told the angry student, "Don't gripe. I'm in a girl sandwich, too!"

Told to get ready to go to preschool, Kyrie', 3, said, "I don't have to. I know it all already!"

Chapter Five

Each child in Mrs. Osterlund's classroom has a 12x15-inch chalkboard for practicing new skills. A basketball coach had given them some old tube socks to use as erasers. When it came time for recess, Mrs. Osterlund showed them how to put their chalk in the sock, roll it up and put it in their desk.

As they were putting on their coats, one of the girls said, "Mrs. Osterlund, I think I'm going to feel funny on the playground this way."

Mrs. Osterlund saw a lump in her sock where she had stuffed her chalk.

Rick asked Alecia, 6, what she was going to do when she grows up.

"Frankly," Alecia told her father, "I haven't had enough peace and quiet to think about it!"

The elementary students had spilled some glitter on the floor. Little Velma noticed it. With her hands on her hips and a gleam in her eyes, Velma announced, "Now that's what I call a shiny floor!"

Mrs. Griebel was reading a book about fish. On one page there were many fish. She asked the preschoolers what a big group of fish is called. They said, "A school."

"I guess that big fish must be the teacher," said Tiffany.

The preschool class was talking about the four food groups. Mrs. Griebel wanted to steer the discussion in the direction of the "fifth" food group, which she calls junk food — foods which taste good but do not help us to grow.

Very seriously, she said, "Children, we need to talk about something very important."

"I know," said Stephen. "We need to talk about motor homes!"

Adam was running late and he couldn't find his shoes. Things would have been desperate, but he thought of a solution. "Mom, I know what to do," he said. "Just stop the clock!"

Catherine, 7, was having a very tough time getting ready for school. It was one of those mornings when everything was going wrong for her.

With infinite patience, her father politely asked if there was anything he could do to help.

"Yes!" she exclaimed. "Make it a Friday night!"

A few days after school started Cathie woke up Dustin, 5, for kindergarten.

He asked her sleepily, "Do I have to go AGAIN?"

Funny Kids

Samuel, 5, gets a quarter a week for doing three chores. One day he had a friend over and started misbehaving. Julia took him aside and told him that if he didn't start behaving, she would take away the quarter she had given him for that week's allowance.

He brought her two quarters and asked, "Which one is it that you gave me? Go ahead and take it away!"

Julia said she didn't know which one she gave him.

"It's the bigger one," he said.

Jeremy said, "I'm the tallest in my class. Who is the tallest in your class, Christopher?"

Christopher thought for a minute and then said, "My teacher."

Kindergarten student Andrew asked his teacher Mary if he could leave and go to Jamie's house to play.

"No, not yet," Mary said. "We still have some school left."

"I have to stay ALL morning?" he asked.

After his first day of kindergarten, Joey told his mother, Wendie, "The teacher calls me by my two names — Joe and Suff." (Joseph)

Mrs. Van Ryn was substitute teaching for a kindergarten class. The regular teacher had left detailed instructions for the schedule for the day. On the chalkboard she had printed in big letters the work "LOOK." In the two Os she had drawn eyes. It was to be the first word the students would learn to read.

Mrs. Van Ryn asked the class if they knew what the letters were. They did. They were all excited as they spelled the word out loud, L-O-O-K.

Then Mrs. Van Ryn asked the class if they knew what the word said. They all agreed they did. So, she said, "OK, class, what does this word say?"

In unison they happily shouted, "See!"

Preschool teacher Mrs. Kelley instructs her children to sit like pretzels with their legs crossed during story time. That way everyone is seated on the floor and everyone can see.

Grant, 5, was sitting with his legs straight out in front of him.

"Don't you know what a pretzel looks like?" Mrs. Kelley asked Grant.

"But Mrs. Kelley," he said. "I like straight pretzels!"

When Mrs. Bower asked Peter how his first week in first grade was, he said, "There's too many rules, and you can't talk."

Chapter Five

The last part of the third-graders' test required them to find four mistakes in a paragraph that talked about Helen Keller and mentioned the movie "The Miracle Worker."

Zech had found three of the mistakes and was desperately searching for the fourth.

Finally, the title "The Miracle Worker" caught his eye. "I know," he shouted triumphantly. "It should be Miracle Whip!"

Mrs. Bolton told her third-graders they needed to pay attention and listen well. One time after she read a story, not one student could answer the questions about the story.

The best student in the class came up to Mrs. Bolton, put her arm around her, and said, "Mrs. Bolton, I DO listen well... But I forget easy!"

When Mrs. Hunter substituted for Mrs. Griebel, she read the children a story about "Curious George." In the story Curious George smokes a pipe. Mrs. Hunter told the students that you should not smoke because it is not good for you.

When Kara asked her son Stephen how preschool had been, he told her that Mrs. Hunter had been his teacher. "She doesn't smoke or ANYTHING!" Stephen said.

After Joey had been in school a few weeks he said, "When you're smart and stupid at the same time, that makes you confused!"

The third-grade class visited Maple Wood Nature Center to learn how maple syrup is made. Part of the lesson was about photosynthesis. While reviewing the lesson, naturalist Scott Beam asked, "What can trees do that we can't do?"

One child answered, "Stand still!"

Mrs. Osterlund's class had a spelling unit in which all the words contained a short e sound. After a long practice session of just spelling the words, she wanted to check comprehension. She asked the children to write down the short e spelling word from their list which would make sense in the sentences she would give them. She started with, "A chicken that lays eggs is a — (hen)."

She glanced across the room and noticed one boy had carefully written "MOM" on his page.

Chapter Six

Kids At Play

"If you want your children to turn out well, spend twice as much time with them, and half as much money," advises Dear Abby. She's right. Children don't need expensive toys. Play that includes things such as imagination, fresh air or exercise can lead to the happiest moments of all.

Seth, 2, saw his older brothers and sister flying kites and asked his dad to help him fly his kite.

Seth handed the Rev. Rittenhouse the string, carried the kite outside, laid it on the patio, flattened it out and sat on it.

Then he said, "OK, Daddy, I ready go for ride!"

Jess told his parents that Greta had fallen down. "She was doing a handstand and let go of the floor," he explained.

Nathan's grandma noticed that he had grass stains on both his knees.

Asked about the stains, Nathan, 6, said, "Well, I'll tell you. I got in a fight and we rolled in the grass. I started the fight, and the teacher made me stand in the corner."

"What did you learn from the punishment?" she asked.

"Never do it while the teacher is watching!" Nathan replied.

Steven and his brother Chad were playing ball. When Steven came in his mother asked who won.

"Well, the score was 7 to more," Steven said. "Chad got 7, and I got more!"

Kristy, 9, went to a garage sale with a friend and returned home with a puppy.

Her mother, Suzie, was shocked and said, "But you didn't have any money!"

"It was free," Kristy said.

In no uncertain terms, Suzie told Kristy that the last thing the family needed was another dog.

"But it's priceless!" Kristy said.

And that's what they named it.

Chapter Six

Paul, 6, started playing PeeWee basketball. One night he ran into the house ahead of his father. He was flushed with excitement.

"Mom, you know what?" he exclaimed. "We played a cribbage game, and we won!"

Paul and I were watching some middle school basketball girls scrimmage. The tiniest girl on the team got fouled.

"She gets TWO!" the coach said. It was the first time that any of the girls had been awarded two free throws.

"Does she get two tries because she's so little?" Paul asked me.

A boy from Taryn's kindergarten class called her at home. "How did he get your number?" Mrs. Mishler asked Taryn.

"I gave it to him," Taryn said.

"Well, don't just give anybody your phone number," Mrs. Mishler said.

"Tomorrow I'll tell him to give it back," Taryn said.

Joshua, 2, went bowling for the first time. On the first try he rolled the ball with a little help and managed to get most of the pins down. His parents yelled, "Yeah, Joshua, you knocked them all down!"

The next time he didn't have the same luck, and his ball ended up in the gutter.

His parents clapped and cheered, "Great job!"

"Yeah, this time I knocked them all up!" Joshua yelled.

Ben, 3, came running into the house bursting with excitement.

"Mom, Mom!" he cried. "Come quick. There's a worm outside that won't let me get on to my swing!"

"What do you mean?"

"It's standing up and sticking its tongue out at me!"

Mrs. McCormick went outside to investigate. She found a garter snake by the swing.

Wendy was trying to get Jacob, 7, to sign up for a summer ball team. She was telling him how much fun he would have.

Little Rebecca overheard the conversation and said, "Jacob, what mom is saying is that you need plenty of fresh air and sunshine."

Funny Kids

Rebecca was playing PeeWee T-ball. There were only two innings per game.

"I'm really enjoying this," she told her mother. "And I know it's good exercise. But Mom, I'm never going to be in the Major League."

Here are some answers from second-graders who competed in St. John Lutheran School's General Knowledge "Quiz Bowl."
Question: What is the liquid that flows through your veins?
Student: GAS!
Question: What is another name for Kris Kringle?
Student: Is he one of the little men on the Rice Krispies box?
Question: Who is our First Lady?
Student: Eve.

While babysitting for his daughter Rachel, 5, Bill went across the road to get the mail. When he got back the phone was ringing.

"This is the sheriff's department," the caller said when Bill answered it. "Do you have a daughter named Rachel?"

"Yes, I do," said Bill. "And I'm looking at her right now."

"She called 911," the lady said, "because she said she couldn't wake up the cat!"

When Adam was told his family was planning a trip to the zoo, he said, "I'm so happy I could bark!"

Nicolas and Janessa were playing doctor with another preschooler. As he looked at pretend X-rays, Nicolas said, "It doesn't look good. We have to take out all your bones!"

"And we're going to take out all your blood!" Janessa added.

Lee was pitching to her grandson Chuck, 5, who was consistently hitting her balls. But after a while he started to miss most of them.

"It looks like your batting average is going down," Lee said.

"Yes," he said, "my batteries are running down."

Suzanna, 9, was filling out her summer camp application. The form asked for first, middle and last name. Suzanna asked her mother, "Do they need my whole name so they know what to call me if I get into trouble?"

Chapter Six

Jess, 2, wanted to come in from playing outside. He called through the screen door, "Dad, I want to come in."

"Well, open the door," Rex said.

"There's a bug."

"Kill it."

"It's too daaaaaaaaaaangerous!" Jess said.

When Rex went to investigate, he found a praying mantis that was over six inches long!

The librarian asked preschooler Cale if he had a library card.

"I don't have a library card," he said. "But I have baseball cards."

Paul had been waiting for weeks for his dad to take him fishing. But when good weather finally came, his father had a bad cold. I told Paul his dad probably couldn't take him because of his cold.

"That doesn't matter," Paul said. "He can take Kleenex."

Olivia was playing inside with her brother's basketball. Jennifer said, "Olivia, the ball is flat. It needs some air."

So Olivia took it outside!

Chapter Seven

The Most Important Thing Is Her Smile

Parents enroll their children in dance classes because they believe dance instruction will help improve their children's confidence, coordination and overall physical fitness. If dance lessons help the child land a part in the school musical some day, well that, too, would be nice. But for little girls there is a more important reason for dance lessons — the lovely costumes they will wear at the recital.

My 6-year-old's recital is Saturday. For weeks now her closet has been bursting with sequins, lace, and cotton candy tutus. The tutus are so fluffy we can't close the closet door. On her shelf is a gold tiara encrusted with so much glitter that gold dust sprinkles down when I pass by.

Elizabeth's dance costumes are the epitomy of her dreams. Like a gourmet contemplating bonbons, she revels in trying to decide which frilly confection she likes better — the red and white polka dot tap ensemble with silver sequins, lace cuffs, perky tutu and big polka dot bow for her hair, or the lavender ballet costume with a foaming tutu, gold sequin striped bodice, sequin and lace collar and the glittering gold tiara.

"I didn't think I'd have anything like this until my WEDDING!" she sighed as I fastened the white lace cuffs of her tap outfit around her outstretched wrists. And I have to admit I felt I was getting a taste of what it will be like to be the mother of the bride.

We began poring over dance catalogs during the dreary winter months. There were a few minor disagreements between adults and students as to what costumes to choose, but, by and large, the children made the decisions. When the outfits arrived in April, everyone was enchanted.

Elizabeth's recital will not be the beginning of an illustrious dance career. The kindest things I can say about her dancing is that she knows her routines, she doesn't fall down (usually) and she has a great smile.

But Saturday we will treat Elizabeth like a prima donna. She will have lipstick, rouge, eye shadow, a splash of perfume and curls courtesy of Aunt Wendy's curling iron. All her relatives living within 15 minutes of the auditorium will be in

Chapter Seven

attendance, and we'll have cake and ice cream at our house afterwards.

The instructor, Pam Isbell, has been a little edgy lately. She knows what can go wrong. So instruction in poise has been added to the curriculum. This is what Elizabeth said Pam told the class last week:

"If your ballet slipper falls off, keep dancing. If your crown falls off, leave it on the stage. If a strap falls down, leave it. But if both straps fall off, hold them up. You're in BIG TROUBLE!"

The students who are performing twice have an additional worry: changing from one spectacular and complicated costume to another. With help from the backstage volunteers, the little girls must change shoes, tights, leotards, tutus, cuffs, collar, tiara and bow. Will they be ready on time for their second performance? Will the crowns be on straight? How much glitter will fall on to their cheeks?

Not that Elizabeth doesn't practice changing clothes. She changes her regular clothes three or four times a day. But her costumes are off limits. Pam said not to wear them until the recital.

But after the recital, Elizabeth will put her costumes on daily. If I know her, she'll mix the costumes and add touches of her own such as a magic wand, my high heels or her little sister's pink feather boa. The fluffy tutus will be used for everything from a bridal veil to sumptuous beds for her dolls.

Although it's annoying when my best gloves or scarves disappear, I enjoy watching Elizabeth and her friends dress up. The clothes of childhood are part of the magic of that time. Childhood is the only time in life when all possibilities are open. A little boy can be a cowboy in the morning, a basketball star after naptime and an astronaut when it's time to blast off for bed. A little girl can dress up and be Queen for a Day. While serving tea and cookies to her dolls (water and Cheerios), she can plan to be a ballet dancer, nurse, kindergarten teacher, Vanna White and Jessica Fletcher (all rolled into one) while being married to Prince Charming and raising seven royal children.

Parents watch and know that all the dreams won't come true. Choices have to be made, and some things are unattainable. But we remember how wonderful it is to feel that everything is possible.

When I watch the dancers Saturday night, everyday problems will leave my mind. I will be with those children in fantasy land. If Elizabeth happens to kick her tap shoe into the audience or twirl into the curtains, Pam may cringe. But I won't care. I'll only be looking for Elizabeth's smile ... and sparkles in her eyes (hopefully not caused by cascading glitter).

I'll be grinning like a Cheshire cat. But I'll have a lump in my throat.

(May 31, 1988)

Chapter Eight

That's My Boy!

Carefree, ornery, logical, energetic, cuddly, unpredictable — all those words describe our wonderful little boys.

Paul's big weakness in kindergarten was his handwriting. While looking at his report card, which listed his writing skills as "unsatisfactory," I said he really had to start working on his handwriting.

"But Mom!" he protested. "I'm going to be a DOCTOR!"

Zachary, 4, rode his bicycle to the barber with his father to get a haircut.

On the way home they rode real fast down a hill, and the wind rushed through his hair.

"Dad, did my new haircut blow off?" he asked anxiously.

Chuck, 4, couldn't believe it when he found out that his sister Lucy's two 4-H pigs were boy pigs.

"But they're pink!" he said.

One time when I stopped by Debbie Rittenhouse's home to discuss the watercolors for this book, I brought Paul, 6. On the way I told Paul that Debbie is an artist. He didn't know what an artist was, so I told him it's someone who paints pictures. And I told him how lucky I was to have Debbie painting pictures for my book.

A few minutes later Paul asked me, "Mom, which is better — a doctor, a scientist or a paintist?"

Jayden, 3, told his parents Lonnie and Cathy, "When I get older I'm gonna be a daddy. That way when you yell at me, I can yell back!"

Mark, 7, and his cousin Sarah, 3, are very close. Every time they greet each other they hug and kiss. One time at a family gathering Sarah was "too busy" to hug Mark.

Dejected, he told his aunt, "I guess I've lost my touch!"

Chapter Eight

We were sitting down to eat in a restaurant. When I looked across the table at Paul, 5, I was shocked to see that his hands had brown and black streaks. Paul seemed oblivious to the dirt.
"What's on your hands?" I asked.
"Fingernails," Paul replied.

Brad told his preschool teacher, Mrs. Griebel, that he was very upset with his father. "You know what Daddy did?" he said. "He put something on our lawn to kill all the dandelions."

Mrs. Griebel was helping Travis write, "MOM."
"How come you know my Mom's name?" Travis asked.

Some birds fluttered around our car on a warm spring day. "I don't like birds," Paul, 5, said with a scowl.
"Why not?" I asked.
"Because they eat worms," he said. "And worms are good for fishing."

Michael, 7, came across some maggots outside.
"Look at those worms," he said.
"Those aren't worms," his mother Angela said. "They are maggots."
"What are maggots?"
"Baby flies."
"You could use those for fishing."
"Nah, you couldn't. They couldn't be bait."
"Yes, you could!" Michael said. "You could use them for fly fishing!"

"Stop that whining!" Vickie told her grandson, Justin, 4. "You're too old to be whining."
"I am not," Justin said. "My mom is 23, and she whines all the time."

Charna and her son Cal, 5, were driving Drew, a fourth-grader, to the Indiana Facts Contest.
"Where are we going?" Cal asked.
"We're going to see Drew answer questions about Indiana," Charna said.
"Football or basketball?" Cal asked.

After a seventh-grade basketball game, Paul, 4, gave the high-five to a number of seventh-grade boys.
"Paul, that was really cool when you gave the high-five to all those boys," Dorothy told him later.
"I didn't high-five," Paul said. "I karate-chopped them!"

Funny Kids

Aaron, 3, was all wound up and running around the house. Suddenly he came up to Carla and said, "Mom, I better sit down. I can hear my heart beeping!"

Colton, 2, took an extra big bite.
"That's too big a bite," Grandpa said.
"I'm making my new teeth work," Colton said.

Vi called Chuck's grandmother to see if she had seen his T-ball hat. Vi said she couldn't believe that Chuck had lost his T-ball hat the first day he had it.
Overhearing the telephone conversation, Chuck corrected his mother. "I lost it the LAST day I had it," he said.

My favorite perfume was sitting at the back of my dresser, gathering dust. Paul, 5, picked it up and said, "Mom, put some of this on."
"No," I said. "I only use it when I get all dressed up."
"Like on Halloween?" he asked.

Mrs. Griebel was talking with her preschoolers about famous dogs. They discussed Snoopy, Clifford the Big Red Dog and Carl the Rottweiler. Mrs. Griebel asked the students if they knew of any other famous dogs.
"Our neighbor has a dog," Stephen said. "He's not famous yet. He's just a puppy!"

"Yes, I'm playing soccer now," Luke, 6, told a little girl. She looked very impressed.
"It's a very dangerous sport," Luke continued. "People get killed out there!"

Chuck, 4, idolizes an older friend at day care. Recently Kyle lost all his front baby teeth. One day when Vi came to pick up Chuck, she saw Chuck running his fingers over his front teeth, obviously envious of the gaping hole in his friend's mouth.
"You have to be in kindergarten to lose your teeth," Kyle told Chuck. "You have to be tough!"

I bought Paul, 6, some new gloves. He put them on and happily buried his face in his gloved hands.
"Are these from Wal-Mart?" he asked.
I said yes.
"I could tell by the SMELL," Paul said.

Chapter Eight

"In about an hour your mom will come and pick you up," I told Dustin, 6, who was playing at our house.

"That's not going to be easy for her to do," Dustin said very seriously. "I weigh 60 pounds."

While swimming, Jeff, 3, saw a pair of swimming trunks at the bottom of the pool.

"There's swimming trunks in the pool," he told his mother. "And NOBODY'S in them!"

Chuck, 4, was getting ready for school. His mother sent him to brush his teeth, and he came back a few seconds later.

"You didn't brush your teeth," she said.

"Yes I did."

"Well, you couldn't have done a very good job because you did it so quickly."

"I didn't want to wear them out!"

Charna was holding her son Cal, 6, and they were listening to the radio. Everything was quiet.

The song, "If I Said You Had A Beautiful Body Would You Hold It Against Me?" came on. Cal listened intently and then turned around, cupped Charna's face in his hands and said, "You've got a beautiful body, Mom!"

Justin, 6, started swimming on the YMCA swim team. He called his Uncle Kevin at Indiana University to tell him about being on the swim team.

"What are you swimming in?" Kevin asked.

"My swimsuit!" Kevin exclaimed. "What do you think I'm swimming in?"

Paul, 4, was intently watching the Wimbledon tennis match between Andre Agassi and Boris Becker. Agassi had a long blond ponytail coming out the back of his white cap, a gold necklace and one dangly gold earring.

"Who are you for?" I asked.

"I'm for the girl!" Paul said emphatically.

When Paul, 5, went to bed he had tears in his eyes because his foot hurt so badly. I told him that it was probably just growing pains.

The next morning he came to me and said very seriously, "I think my foot shrunk last night. Let's measure it."

Funny Kids

Vi was cuddling 2-year-old Jeff and telling him what a good boy he was.

He wrapped his arms around her and gave Vi a big hug. "You're a good boy, too," he said.

Vi Sutton, the aunt of this book's author, took Richard, 6, shoe shopping. He tried on a pair of shoes, but another pair caught his eyes.

"Well, let's try one of these on, and then you can make up your mind," the salesman said. "But first you have to take off one of your shoes."

"Yes, or grow another foot mighty fast!" Richard said.

Every time Lori took her son Michael, 4, shopping she told him she was broke so that he wouldn't pester her to buy things for him.

One day as they walked toward the store he found a penny on the ground.

He picked it up, handed it to her and said, "Here, Mommy, now you are fixed!"

Chapter Nine

The World According to Kids

A "kid's eye view" of the world is refreshing.

Rachelle, 4, and Justin, 2, came from Wisconsin to visit cousins in Indiana.

They were playing on the swingset in the backyard, when suddenly they came running to the house screaming, "Auntie Sue! Auntie Sue!"

Sue met them at the door expecting to see blood and broken bones protruding out of the skin. "What's wrong? What happened?" she asked.

"The clouds! The clouds!" the children exclaimed.

"What about the clouds?"

"THEY'RE MOVING! THEY'RE MOVING!"

"They're supposed to move."

"But they don't move in Wisconsin!"

The Coles lost their home in the July 14, 1992 tornado that struck Kendallville. As friends were trying to help clean things up, there was a moment of silence as everyone looked at the mess in amazement.

Then Lindsay, 5, broke the silence by saying, "Those darn tornadoes don't even watch where they're going, do they?"

Chuck, 5, was watching the Chain O' Lakes parade in Albion. Marching in the parade were some veterans. His mother explained to him that veterans are people who fought in wars to protect our nation, and that is why we honor them.

As he watched the veterans march by, Chuck asked, "Are those the ones who didn't die?"

When the preschoolers were talking about animals Travis displayed a duck calling device that he had brought from home. After showing it to his classmates, he demonstrated it.

"What does the hunter use the duck call for?" Mrs. Griebel asked.

"He calls the ducks so that he can pet them," Travis said.

Chapter Nine

Matthew was was being driven home from preschool when he commented, "I wonder where the clouds come from and where they go."

About a month later when he was again being driven home from preschool, they passed Newnam Manufacturing, which has a big smokestack.

"THAT'S where the clouds come from," he said.

When the Rittenhouse children were younger, they each received a goldfish. One by one the fish died, until Ben's was the only one left.

One day Ben, 5, came to his mother and said, "Mommy, come look at my goldfish. It's taking a nap on the bottom of the bowl!"

Cody, 8, was very worried that President George Bush would lose his bid for re-election, because then Bush would be out of a job. Cody kept pestering his mother to vote for Bush. But she kept telling Cody she hadn't made up her mind yet.

"Well, you know, Mom," Cody said. "George Bush really hasn't done such a bad job. We've only had one war and two hurricanes!"

Stevie's mother is a single parent. One day when she picked him up from kindergarten he was very upset.

"Mom, Kevin said you were the tooth fairy," Stevie said.

"That's right," his mother said. And she tried to explain to him. But Stevie just got angrier. "Why are you so mad to find out that I'm the tooth fairy?" she asked.

"You never told me I was alone at night while you were out collecting teeth!" Stevie replied.

"This just isn't your day," Angela's mother said when the 4-year-old fell down.

The next day Angela hurt herself again, and again her mother's words of comfort ended with, "This just isn't your day."

"Well, whose day is it, anyway?!" Angela asked.

Liz, 10, used to say she wanted to be an actress and live in New York City. But then she changed her mind. She announced she still wants to be an actress, but she doesn't want to live in New York City because there is too much crime there.

She said she wants to live in Los Angeles instead!

During a trip to the zoo, Darrin, 3, said, "When I grow up, I want to be a monkey, eat bananas and hang from the trees!"

Funny Kids

As a special treat, the Suttons took their daughter Jane, 5, to New York City. They stayed in the elegant Plaza Hotel and took in all the typical tourist sights: Empire State Building, Central Park, famous stores, etc. On their drive back to Delaware they asked Jane, "Of all the sights in New York City, what did you like best?"

Evidently, it was the hotel that made the biggest impression on her, because she replied: "The chandelier in the elevator!"

One day DeWayne told his teacher Mrs. Osterlund that Marilyn was his cousin. Mrs. Osterlund was surprised. She asked whose mother and whose father were sister and brother, or whether their mothers were sisters. She kept getting negative answers. Finally she said, "Oh, you must be distant cousins."

DeWayne looked at her with a puzzled expression. "No, just about four miles down the road," he said.

Chuck, 3, was roasting in the back seat of the family car because of the afternoon sun. He angrily told his mother that when he got home he was going to shoot the sun down.

After a moment of thought, he asked, "If the sun falls on me, will I get a sunburn?"

Paul, 6, was in the Tropical Treasures Pet Shop with his big sister Dorothy. Paul struck up a conversation with a parrot. The conversation consisted of a series of hellos from the parrot to Paul and from Paul to the parrot.

After a while Paul asked Dorothy if she were going to buy the robot bird.

"That's not a robot. It's a real bird," Dorothy said.

"No, it's a robot," Paul said. "Birds can't talk."

Jonathan, 4, brought a worm to his mother. It was wiggling on his hand.

"Mom, this worm is petting me," Jonathan said.

In a catalog Brittany, 4, saw a picture of a table and chairs decorated like black and white Holstein cows.

"Mom, there's a dalmatian cow!" Brittany exclaimed.

Taryn, 4, learned a friend of the family's was going to be on the Hoosier lottery show. The friend asked Taryn if she was going to watch him on TV.

She thought for a minute and said, "Yes, and I'm going to change the channels until you get dizzy!"

Chapter Nine

Mrs. Becker took Andrew, 3, to every bargain sale, clearance sale, garage sale and double coupon day.

One day as Mrs. Becker and Andrew drove past the IGA, she saw that they were having a tent sale.

"Oh, I forgot IGA was having a tent sale today," she said.

Andrew piped up, "Well, you better hurry up, Mom. They only have one left!"

When Todd was 8 his parents were getting ready for a garage sale. His dad asked his mom what to do with the price for an old table. She said just put $20 on the table.

Todd looked at his parents and said, "It'll never work. Someone will just take the $20 and leave that old table!"

Erika, 3, was examining a nickel with her father. "That's George Washington," she said. And turning the nickel over, she said, "And that's his house!"

Josh and Gary were sharing a soft drink when Josh burped.
"What do you say?" Gary asked.
"I'm sorry," Josh said.
"No, you should say 'excuse me.'"
"'Excuse me' means get out of the way."
"No, 'excuse me' means 'pardon me, I'm sorry for what I have done. Please excuse me.'"
"No, that means I pushed you!"

Kaleb, 5, asked, "Mommy, what does 'I beg your pardon' mean?"
"That's a polite way to say 'What?' or 'Say that again.'"
"No!" Kaleb said. "That's what you say when you need Beltone (hearing aids)!"

Christopher, 4, was watching an elderly man bag his mother's groceries. He watched the gentleman intently as he took the groceries to the car and unloaded them.

When he got to the car, Christopher said, "Mom, did you know that man is part robot?"

"Why do you say that?"

"Because he has those things (hearing aids) in his ears!"

"Do you know what this is? It's a subway, but not the kind you can eat!"

Funny Kids

Mitch, 7, sadly told Chuck, 5, that he had sold his Nolan Ryan baseball card last year to his uncle for $1.

"Why did you sell it?" Chuck asked.

"I was young then," Mitch sighed. "I thought a buck was good money."

Cathie, the mother of two, was homebound because Scott, 2, was in the midst of a case of chicken pox. When I called Cathie, Dustin, 6, answered the phone.

I asked to speak to Cathie. Then I heard squeals from Scott. "I want to talk to her. I want to talk to her," Scott said.

"You CAN'T talk to her," Dustin said. And I heard him wrestle the receiver from Scott. "We don't know for sure if she has had the chicken pox yet!"

Over the years Paul's favorite blanket became smaller and smaller. There was so little of it left, that one of his sisters said, "It's so little that he could floss with it!"

David was in the park with his babysitter, Mrs. Maxson, when he saw a long-legged Great Blue Heron.

"Look at that Michael Jordan bird!" he said.

On the way to the store a 4-year-old saw a dead cat by the side of the road. He got a sad look on his face and said, "It didn't look both ways!"

Joey, 4, always complained when his daddy left for work at Wauseon Machine and Manufacturing Inc.

"Daddy has to go to work to make money," his parents would tell him over and over.

One day his father brought home a piece of a part he was making to show Joey what he does at work.

"This is what I make at work," Mike said.

"No," Joey said. "You make money!"

Naomi was talking with David, 7, about how the Earth is continually rotating and moving around the sun.

A lightbulb turned on in David's head. "No wonder sometimes we get dizzy!" he exclaimed.

Chapter Nine

Jamison, 5, got a puppy that was a mix of German Shepherd and Akita. He kept forgetting what two breeds his puppy was, and Ingrid kept having to tell him over and over again. One day after she had told him, Jamison thought a minute and said, "I think the back half is German Shepherd and the front half is Akita."

A 7-year-old was taken to the sale barn in the small farming community of Topeka. He had never seen Amish people before.

His eyes grew big. It was very silent until he exclaimed, "Look at all those pilgrims."

The Amish all laughed.

Chapter Ten

And the Band Played On

The letter to parents of fifth-graders contained a compelling quote from Aristotle: "Since music has so much to do with the molding of character it is necessary that we teach it to our children."

Not being musicians ourselves, my husband and I didn't know what to expect when we said "OK" to our oldest child's pleas to be in the middle school band.

At the student-parent information night in April, band leaders Peter Bottomley and James Swartzlander told parents how beneficial the band experience would be for our youngsters. The child who learns to play an instrument learns discipline, cooperation with others and a new way to a fuller, richer life, they said. An instrument automatically places a child in worthwhile school activities and provides something interesting and pleasurable to do during leisure time, they added.

As I listened to them describe the merits of music, I felt the catch in my throat I get whenever I watch a marching band. And I tried to imagine the youngsters in uniform.

For weeks Dorothy debated which instrument to play. She repeatedly asked my opinion, but I couldn't help because I barely knew what each instrument was called, much less what it would sound like or how much it would cost to rent.

But at the private conference with the band equipment salesman, I learned the choice was obvious.

Dorothy, we found out, is gifted for playing the trombone. Nearly the tallest girl in her class, she is one of the few students her age who has arms long enough to extend the slide. She is a born trombone player!

Father, who had been at home babysitting when we made this discovery, greeted us at the door.

"What are you going to play?" he and the three kids asked eagerly. We told them to sit around the kitchen table for the announcement.

When everyone was quiet, Dorothy and I said in happy unison: "The trombone!"

"AAARRGH!" father screamed, burying his face in his hands.

I guess he wanted the flute.

The doubts certain family members had about the wisdom of our choice were eased when the trombone came home during the first week of school. It looked magnificent! And Dorothy looked magnificent holding it.

Chapter Ten

She spent happy hours polishing the gleaming brass with Windex and flannel, oiling the slide, disinfecting the mouthpiece with Listerine, vacuuming the plush insides of the case, and chasing her siblings away from the golden, glowing instrument that they were not allowed to breath on or touch.

After Dorothy made her choice last spring, my friend who plays the clarinet congratulated me, claiming the trombone is one of the least objectionable instruments to listen to while a child is learning to play. I was relieved.

But, frankly, when Dorothy started practicing we wondered if she would ever be able to play in public. I cannot politely describe the sounds that exploded from her horn. The mating calls of wild elephants are tame compared to her eruptions.

When she played for the paternal grandparents in October, they managed to listen without covering their ears.

"Dolly, I don't mean to be disrespectful," Grandma said hesitantly when Dorothy had exhausted her repertoire and her audience. "But when is it going to sound like... uh... music?"

Dorothy just smiled and spent extra time polishing that night.

A month later, at the first sixth-grade band concert, the auditorium was nearly full of parents, grandparents and siblings — even though there were only 40 students in the sixth-grade band. I suspect they were all secretly doubting that anything worthy of the name music could come from the well-scrubbed kids nervously assembled on stage.

I was uneasy for several reasons. Some of Dorothy's songs still resembled jungle sounds to me. Also, Mr. Swartzlander had told Dorothy that at a sixth-grade concert several years ago a trombone player's slide fell off. Since putting a slide back on is a major job, if that happened to Dorothy, it would leave the entire trombone section incapacitated for the rest of the night. The other trombone player had been sick all week.

Also, Dorothy was wearing dress shoes a size too small for her. Up until a half hour before curtain time, I had assumed she would wear her new school shoes. But at the last minute she said they weren't up to "Swartzlander-Bottomley" standards and insisted on wearing too-small dress shoes, which, I feared, might impair her air flow.

After the first 30-second piece, I started breathing again. Dorothy and her trombone were still intact.

Actually, listening to music was what we did the least of that night. We spent much more time listening to the band directors explain what they had tried to accomplish during the first weeks of instruction, applauding thunderously after each short piece and enjoying refreshments in the cafeteria afterwards.

But — and this is the amazing part — what we heard WAS music, not jungle sounds! Father said it was just the kind of concert he likes — short. The younger siblings thought the cookies were wonderful.

Dorothy, limping slightly, looked as relieved as I was.

(Nov. 21, 1990)

"Here's the police! Everyone put their seatbelts on!"

"Wow, that guy had on strong aftershave lotion!
I could smell it clear through the phone!"

Chapter Eleven

Bathroom Humor

Potty training is one of the least favorite aspects of parenthood. The best way to get through potty training is to look for the humor in it. One mother remembers the first time her son went into the men's restroom on his own. She thought everything was fine, until she heard a call that echoed through the restaurant, "Mommy, come and wipe me off!"

With little modesty and lots of pride in their potty training adventure, children don't think twice about using potty-related words, no matter what the situation.

A urologist, Dr. Nancy Hockley works long hours. One night she came home absolutely exhausted. Sarah, 4, ran to her mother demanding attention, but Nancy was too tired to respond.
"Your mother's pooped," Norman said.
"Where?!" Sarah asked with amazement, looking over her shoulder.

Ron was watching TV when a commercial came on advertising taking schooling at home. "Act now," the actress urged. Her voice rose. "Begin training at once in your home for one of these careers."
"Quit saying that," Ron said, his voice rising, too. "I AM trained. I can go to the bathroom by myself!"

When George and his son Michael, 2, were at Grandma Haynes' house, George needed to use the restroom. Shortly after George entered the bathroom, Michael started knocking on the door, asking to be let in.
"I'll be out in a minute," George replied.
After knocking three times and hearing the same reply, Michael said, "I'll blow your house down!"

Jess was visiting his grandmother, Mrs. Jansen. He had just gotten out of diapers. One day she heard a knock on the bathroom door.
"Are you in there, Grandma?"
"Yes, Jess."
"Are you standing up or sitting down?"

Chapter Eleven

Amanda, 5, checked with her mother before going to the restaurant restroom. Assured that she should use the restroom with the most letters on the door or the one with a dress shape, she confidently left.

But a few minutes later she came back. Her distraught voice announced to all, "I can't go. It's chickens!"

The Cripes had been redecorating their bathroom. Jessica Allyson, 3, walked in and looked at the bare black floor with all the linoleum scraped off.

"Where did the OTHER bathroom go?" she asked.

Lucy, 9, was telling her mother about how much fun her younger brothers were having playing in the bathtub.

"You can tell I'm getting older," Lucy said. "I get BORED when I take my bath."

Ingrid was giving her new baby Seth a bath, under the watchful eyes of older brother Jamie, 6.

When Ingrid brushed Seth's hair, some cradle cap was noticeable.

"What's chipping away his head?!" Jamie asked in alarm.

Errin, 2, was being potty trained. After she was done going potty, she asked her mother, "Mommy, can you sweep my bottom?"

Deb Cooper was getting ready to wash and wax her kitchen floor. She told her three boys to use the bathroom, because they couldn't come back through the kitchen until the floor was dry.

That night the Cooper family went for a ride with their grandparents. They passed a house with a port-a-potty in the front yard.

"I wonder why they have a port-a-potty in their front yard," Deb said.

"Do you suppose their mom is mopping the floor?" Cory, 10, asked.

Jon was driving with his son Ethan, 3. Out of the blue, Ethan asked, "Dad, do you know what?"

"No, what?"

"We are people because we can see and poop!" Ethan announced.

Shawn, 3, was finally having success with potty training, so his parents were continually telling him how proud they were of him for using "the big potty."

One day Shawn saw his father come out of the restroom. Shawn came running to him and hugged his legs. "I'm so proud of you!" he told his dad. "You went potty on the big potty!"

Funny Kids

A family was watching the movie "Schindler's List" which is nearly six hours long. At one point in the movie the back of a man who is urinating is shown. The family's daughters were shocked by the scene.

But the family's little boy was not surprised or shocked. He told his sisters, "It's a long movie. He had to go sometime."

The Herricks' neighbors were fertilizing the garden with manure. The boys begged to go out and watch the neighbor unload the dump truck. Sue told them they could go outside if they stayed out of the way. But the boys were soon back in the house. Sue asked them why they didn't stay out longer.

"Someone passed some really bad gas!" Matt said.

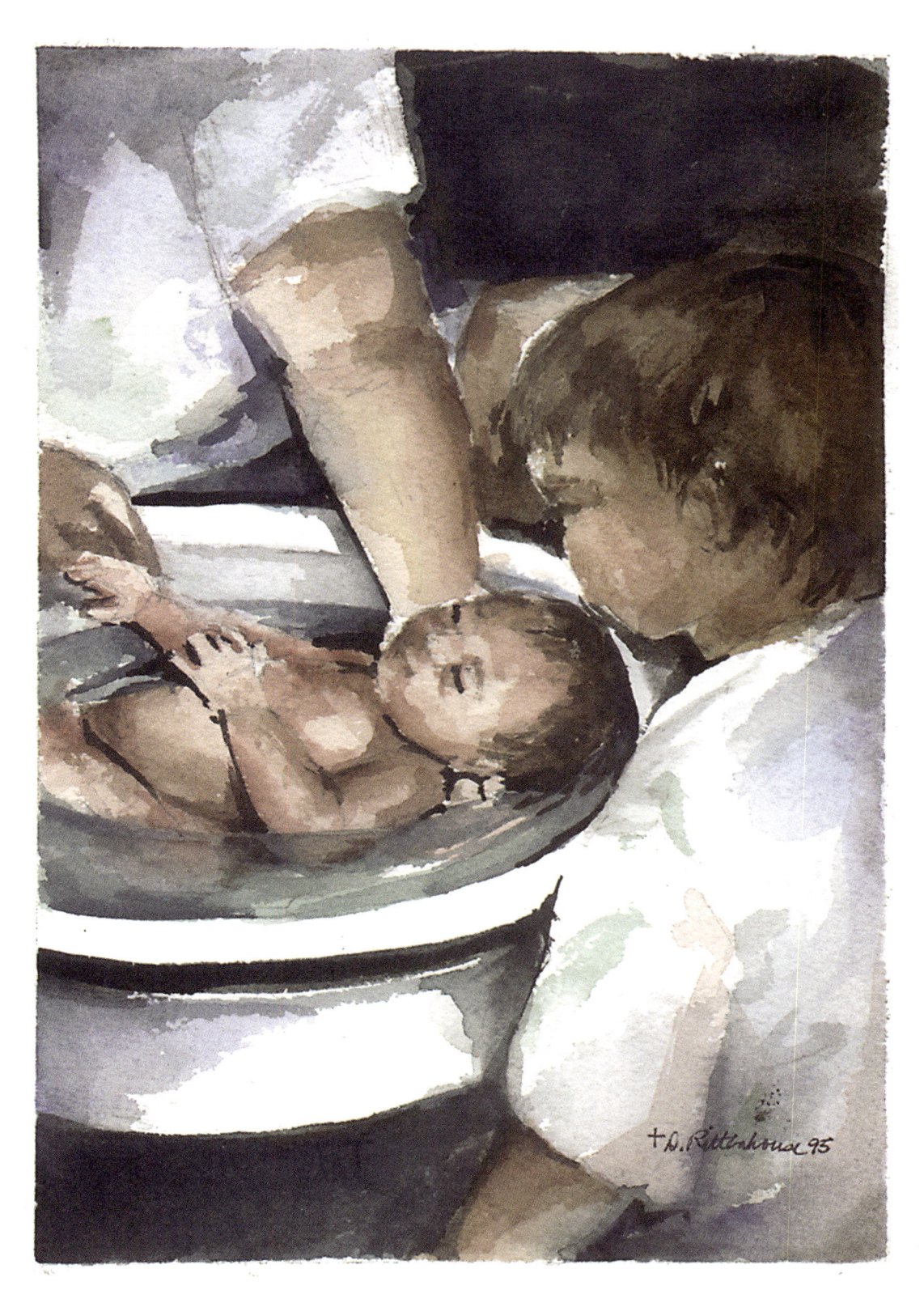

"What's chipping away his head?"

Told his batting average was going down,
Chuck said, "Yes, my batteries are running down!"

Chapter Twelve

Dressing For Success

"Clothes make the man. Naked people have little or no influence in society."

Attributed to Mark Twain

My baby advice book says infants don't need real shoes until they begin to walk. Until that age — about 1 year — the sole (no pun intended) function of shoes is to keep the socks on.

Keeping socks on is a problem because infants have a fascination with their toes. Pulling off their socks to get to their toes is one of babies' favorite pastimes. Then they stuff the socks into their mouth, so that they become too soggy to put back on. Naked, waving feet are fine in most situations, but sometimes, such as on chilly days or during a wedding, naked feet are not acceptable.

My baby advice book suggests postponing the purchase of real shoes until the child is ready to walk. Until then, the book says, you should buy the most inexpensive foot covering you can find. But the author, a male, overlooks a mother's deep-rooted emotions about shoes.

When Paul was 7 months old I could hold out no longer. Even though he probably wouldn't be walking for six or seven more months (his three sisters all started walking at 14 months of age), I decided it was time for real shoes.

"Do you want high tops?" the clerk at Taylor's asked.

"Well, not exactly," I said. What I meant was I wanted my son's first pair of shoes to be different from my daughters' first pairs. The clerk seemed to understand.

She measured his slender foot. After a long search in the back room, she brought out a pair of white and blue high top Nikes, size 3. They had all the detailing of the Nikes worn by the pros. The clerk easily slipped them on Paul, who was so startled he didn't have time to kick or curl up his toes.

Dangling at the end of Paul's bird-like legs, the shoes looked huge. We decided there was a good chance they would last until he took his first steps.

I noticed a sticker on the sole of one of the shoes. It said "No Mark."

"What's that?" I asked, wondering if it was some new kind of union label.

"That means they won't mark gym floors," the clerk said, peeling it off.

I left the shoes on Paul and paid for them. As I buttoned him back into his jacket, I thought he looked older. The Nikes had turned him from a baby into a lit-

Chapter Twelve

tle boy. Mark Twain's observation that "clothes make the man" fluttered through my mind.

At home Paul was not dismayed at having his toes held hostage. He had new playthings — the foot-long laces. And the colorful leather uppers and thick rubber soles were nice for teething.

As I watched him lie on his back and coo at his Nikes, I thought of all the dreams that are expressed in little boys' clothes. From the day he was born, Paul has been dressed in outfits that labeled him as a sea captain, a pro football or basketball player, a fireman, "Champ," "Little Slugger," etc. A dress jacket, white shirt, suspenders and clip-on tie are waiting for him in the back of the closet. All he needs is a briefcase to look perfectly dressed on Wall Street.

Only 7 months old and just learning to crawl Paul is wearing Nikes guaranteed not to mark the gym floor. Whoever made his shoes must think it's a real possibility that he might leap from my arms, race wildly down the gym floor and slam-dunk a basketball, just like the picture of the player on his "All Pro" sweatshirt.

I hold him tighter and think of the dreams that are wrapped up in little boys' clothes.

(March 22, 1988)

Chapter Thirteen

Kids and the Birds and the Bees

Parents should answer their children's questions about sex honestly. But no matter how careful they are with their explanations, they will probably have to clear up some big mix-ups along the way.

Emalee, 9, and Heather, 8, went with their dad to take their very pregnant boxer, Sadie, to the veterinarian. The girls were in the room when the vet did a very thorough examination of Sadie.

Arriving home, Emalee got "nose to nose" with her mom and said, "You can forget EVER being a grandmother, 'cause I'm NEVER having puppies!"

Emalee and Heather were home when Sadie began to deliver her puppies. As the first pup was born, Emalee yelled for her mom to come quick and see how each pup was born "in its own little baggie."

From the other room, Heather asked, "Are they zip-lock?"

Autumn was 2 when she first noticed her mother's scar from her Cesarean section.

"What's that?" she asked.

"That's where the doctor cut open my belly to take you out," Mrs. Bange said.

"Oh, Mama," Autumn said with deep remorse. "I sorry I crawled in there!"

New parents Vernie and Jane Scheiber were visiting with their niece Devona, 11.

Devona was admiring baby Carrie and trying to decide who the 4-month-old looked like.

"I think she looks like you, Uncle Vern," Devona said. Then she turned to Jane and said, "And she looks a little like you, Aunt Jane. I guess she's a mixture. If she were a dog, I think you'd call her a mutt!"

Chapter Thirteen

When my mom was 5 and her sister Sally was 4 they learned from their mother that babies grow from an egg inside the mother.

One day the two little girls had an argument. Sally was sure she was right. "Oh," she told her older sister, "I knew all about that before you were even an egg!"

Terrie was teasing Nicki, 6, about which came first, the chicken or the egg. When Nicki said the egg, Terrie asked where the egg came from and when Nicki said the chicken, Terrie asked where the chicken came from.

Finally, they were back to the egg. "Where did it come from?" Terrie asked.

"The grocery store!" Nicki said in exasperation.

Terrie told Jonathan, 3, that a lady he knew had her baby.

"She swallowed a baby in her tummy," Jonathan said, remembering how large the woman's abdomen had been.

"Yes, she had her baby, and it was a little girl," Terrie said.

Jonathan's eyes got wide. "She puked it up!" he exclaimed.

Brittany, 3, wanted to see the day-old kittens.

"No, not now, They are eating," Mrs. Becker said.

"What are they eating?" Brittany asked.

Mrs. Becker said they were drinking their mama's milk.

"How do they get their mama's milk?" Brittany asked.

"You know all those bumps on Midnight's tummy," Mrs. Becker replied. "That's where they get their mama's milk."

"Does she have Pepsi ones, too?" Brittany asked.

One evening Mrs. Conley, who was pregnant, told Jayden that she couldn't play with him because her stomach was upset.

"I bet that's because the baby is crying in there," Jayden said.

Joey knows that if a person eats too much he gets fat. He also knows that if a woman is pregnant, she gets fat.

One day out of the blue he asked his mother, "So how much food do you have to eat before it makes a baby?"

Mrs. Becker said the kittens get their milk from the bumps on Midnight's tummy. "Does she have Pepsi ones, too?"

"No gravy today. I want naked potatoes!"

Funny Kids

A neighbor asked if Aaron, 3, wanted a brother or a sister. Aaron didn't utter a word during the conversation, so Gretchen spoke up and said, "I don't think he'd be disappointed with whatever we have."

On their walk home, Aaron said, "Mommy, I will too be disappointed if it's a girl. I want a brother. If it's a girl I'm going to put it back in your tummy!"

The Smurrs' baby was due Oct. 27. Lori told Christopher, 3, that the baby would come at Halloween when the pumpkins in the garden were big and orange.

Every day Christopher went out to inspect the garden.

One day he came to Lori with excitement and said, "Them pumpkins are really big and really orange. You better get to the hospital now!"

Mrs. Hunter heard that Holly, the mother of Klanci, 4, was expecting.

"Are you going to get a new brother or sister in your family?" Mrs. Hunter asked.

"No, I think I'll keep my old ones!" Klanci said.

Before Mary's brother was born, a friend of the family's had a baby, so they took Mary to see the baby at the hospital.

As they were leaving from the nursery window, Mary said, "Just think, Mom. Pretty soon we can come up here and pick our baby out, too!"

Alicia was watching television with her mother when the incredible, edible egg commercial came on.

"If you'd eat more eggs, I could have a baby brother!" Alicia told her mother.

Chris was sitting on his mother's lap. "Mom, I want a kiss," he said.

Nancy gave him a kiss.

"No, Mom," Chris said. "I want a 'twist and kiss' like they do on TV on your shows (soap operas)!"

Phillip wanted a brother. He told his Grandma Diann and Grandma Mary that if Mommy had a sister they could have her and he would take a brother.

But when Phillip did see his brother, he looked right at his mom and said, "Mom, that's a baby — not a brother!"

Chapter Thirteen

When Betty Bower's family was dairy farming in Wisconsin, her sister's family came to visit. Betty's husband needed to put a cow in a pen with the bull for breeding. He asked his brother-in-law if he wanted his 8-year-old son to leave the barn. The brother-in-law decided there was no better time than the present to get the children used to farm life.

He explained to the boy that Uncle Dave was going to put the cow in the same pen with the bull, and the bull was going to plant a seed in the cow and that would make a calf.

When the 8-year-old's mother came to the barn to check on him, he ran to her and said, "Now, mother, don't worry about that cow in the pen with the bull. He won't hurt her. He is going to plant a seed in her, and that will turn into a calf. SEE, she is getting LITTLER already!"

A pregnant mother was telling her 5-year-old about the baby that was growing inside her. She pointed to various parts of her abdomen and said, "Here's the head. Here's the feet, etc."

Later the 5-year-old asked, "If the head is over here and the feet over there, who's going to put her together when they come out?"

Chapter Fourteen

Kids and Marriage

Children have many misunderstandings about tying the knot. These stories are examples of how tangled things can get!

The Osterlund girls went with their parents to a wedding. The next day Mrs. Osterlund noticed Krista and Holly performing a wedding ceremony for their dolls. Holly was the minister.

"Do you take this man to be your awful-headed husband?" was the question asked of the pretend bride.

Mrs. Huelsenbeck overheard the following conversation between two YMCA preschoolers:

"Will you be my wife today?" John Michael asked Talia.

"No," Talia said.

"Why not? You were on Tuesday!"

Branden, 7, was told by his mother that she was expecting a baby, and he would have a new brother or sister.

After some thought, Branden asked, "Does Dad know about this?"

For show and tell Alecia brought Sparkle-haired Barbie. When he saw the doll, Nicolas looked smitten.

"If she was real," Nicolas said, "she would be my wife!"

Many years ago the Banges had alyssum flowers growing in their yard. One day Mrs. Bange noticed a large amount of them had been torn up.

Then she saw that Dina, 4, had stuffed her shirt with the alyssum.

"I'm going to marry David Cassidy and everyone knows you need a bosom to get married!" Dina said.

Rob leaned over to Brittany and asked, "Will you marry me?"

"No," Brittany said. "I have to marry a bigger boy."

"Oh," said Rob, looking very disappointed.

"Oh, OK," said Brittany. "Maybe I will marry you."

Chapter Fourteen

Preschoolers Nicolas and Lacey have decided that when they grow up they are going to get married.

One day when the class was talking about farms, Nicolas said, "When I get big I'm going to live on a farm and get up early to milk the cows."

Lacey, who was sitting next to him, piped up, "Well, don't wake me up!"

Matt, almost 3, was very upset that he wasn't asked to be in his uncle's wedding. They told him he was too little. So he took his mother into the dining room and showed her his baby picture and said, "See, I little then. I have no hair and no teeth."

Then he took her into the kitchen and showed her a picture of himself when he had just turned 2 and said, "See I bigger there."

Then he pointed to himself and said, "I bigger now. I not little anymore. Why can't I be in the wedding?"

Brian, 5, was lying down resting with his mother Julie. Looking at the pictures on the wall, he saw a photograph of his parents that was taken on their honeymoon in Hawaii.

"Where did you get that picture taken? Was it at the zoo?" Brian asked.

"No, it was taken in Hawaii while Mommy and Daddy were on their honeymoon," Julie said.

"When people go on their honeymoon can they choose anywhere in the world to go?" Brian asked.

"Yes, I suppose they can," Julie said.

"Then why didn't you choose Chuck E Cheese?" asked Brian.

A 6-year-old boy had a crush on a girl in his kindergarten class. Finding out about it, his three older sisters started teasing him unmercifully.

"Have you kissed her?" one sister asked.

"NO!"

"Have you held her hand?" another asked.

"NO!"

Then after a moment he said, "But I touched her chair!"

Sue's husband came in while she was preparing lunch. He turned her away from the stove and started waltzing around the room.

Jake giggled and Matt looked terribly worried.

After the dance was over, Matt said, "I don't think that's legal."

"Do you take this man to be your awful-headed husband?"

Funny Kids

When Nick was in first grade there was a discussion in class about mothers. With enthusiasm Nick told about how his mom fixes good food, takes them places and helps them.

Then he finished, "And she's the favorite wife of my dad!"

Out of the blue Dustin, 5, told his mother, "If I find a girl willing to marry me, you know what I'm going to do? Marry her!"

Deidre heard her Aunt Janet went to a shower. "Why did she go to a shower?" Deidre asked. "Did hers quit working?"

Gary, who was going to be married in a few weeks, was talking with his neighbor, Josh, 5.

"I'm never going to get married!" Josh said.

"Why not?" Gary asked.

"Marriage stinks!"

"Why do you say that?"

"Because you have to kiss in front of people!"

Chapter Fifteen

Teaching About Money Takes All the Cents You Have

"Money is flat and meant to be piled up."
Scottish proverb

A galloping case of gold fever has struck our two oldest children.

The question, "How much will you pay me?" is part of their daily vocabulary, and I'm beginning to fear that they'll never do anything for altruistic reasons again.

The two have become acquisitive for different reasons.

The 8-year-old seeks to amass money so that she can count it, stack it, run it through her fingers and put it in — and remove it from — her billfold and piggy bank. She gloats over her growing purchasing power and dreams of her next trip to a discount store.

The 5-year-old is charmed by the thought of her ballooning bank account. She collects pennies, nickels and dimes in an envelope, depositing her money just before the worn paper is about to tear. She loves the idea of interest making her money grow, although her comprehension of the speed at which this happens is fuzzy.

The 8-year-old has quite a bit more in her savings account than the 5-year-old. The first time the two went to the bank together, the 8-year-old deposited her money first. The 5-year-old didn't put hers in until a few minutes later.

"I have more money than you," the 8-year-old boasted that night.

The 5-year-old was unperturbed. "That's because you put your money in first," she responded, attributing their difference in savings to rampantly compounding interest and not to their difference in birth order.

The dilemma that gold fever poses to me is whether to put the two girls on an allowance and stop paying on a fee for service basis. I dole out small change for chores such as playing with the 2-year-old, picking up toys or cleaning out closets and drawers. An allowance might be simpler, but I could lose leverage.

There are days when the two come begging for helpful things to do. Their active imaginations work overtime dreaming up jobs.

"Mom, can I watch Catherine?" the 5-year-old asked the other day, just after her younger sister had been put down for a nap.

Chapter Fifteen

"Not now," I replied. "She's sleeping."

"Well, I'll watch her sleep," the 5-year-old responded, dollar signs in her eyes.

The inflation rate is another reason I lean against allowance. When I was 5 I started out with a 25 cent stipend. That was when we lived in Pine Orchard, Connecticut. When we moved to New York City and family finances were tight, I was cut to 10 cents. I remember saving for weeks to buy my first billfold and then having nothing to put in it.

My children would sneer at a 10 cent or 25 cent allowance. A recent Associated Press story reported the average American child gets an allowance of $3.34 a week, with 5-year-olds starting at $1.40. It's hard for me to imagine giving away $3 or $4 a week — unless I made them buy their own Happy Meals.

I need to start talking with them about helping around the house just to be nice and about budgets — mine in particular. I need to make the 8-year-old understand that just because you have money, that doesn't mean it can be spent on anything you like. She must realize my billfold is not bottomless.

I remember our first conversation about money four years ago. An expensive stuffed toy was advertised on television. The then 4-year-old wanted me to order it.

"I don't have the money," I told her.

"Write a check," she commanded.

Somehow we parents need to instill some sense of fiscal responsibility in our children. I wish I could give some advice on exactly how that can be done, but I'm still trying to figure it out myself.

If parents succeed, I can imagine a major turn-around in our national debt problem. Children who know you can't just "write a check" might turn into voters who look askance at politicians who solve problems by simply printing more money.

Looking back at the allowance vs. payment for servie dilemma — maybe we voters have chosen the wrong approch. Would we have more clout if we withheld salaries until our lawmakers could show us real progress on the tasks they promised to tackle?

If we raise our children right, maybe someday there will be more sense in Washington as well as more cents in the taxpayers' pockets.

Meanwhile, I need to start supper for my family. But before I begin, I think I'll give my two oldest daughters some food for thought. I'll ask each one, "How much will you pay me?" and threaten to give dinner only to the highest bidder.

(Aug. 18, 1987)

Chapter Sixteen

There's No Such Thing As a Foolish Question

Sometimes children's continual "whys" drive parents crazy. But children who don't get the brush-off, who get their questions answered honestly and accurately, are on their way to becoming intelligent adults. It really is true that there is no such thing as a foolish question — but there are funny questions!

When Adam was 6 he asked his father, "Dad, how old do I have to be before I can talk about the good old days?"

While Richard and his Grandmother Hulett were enjoying a nice fall day, they saw an old jack-o-lantern, all shriveled up and broken from the top of its head to its nose.

Richard looked up at his grandmother and asked, "Would you say that pumpkin has a splitting headache?"

When the Rasps figured out that their cat, Noah, has lived so long that if he were a human he would be 98 years old, Rebecca, 4, asked, "Does Noah know he is an adult?"

Adam, 4, was walking through the woods with his stepfather. Because it was Adam's first trip in nature, his stepfather pointed out things of interest.

They came upon a deer stand in a tree. Adam looked at his stepfather with a puzzled expression and asked, "How do the deer get up there?"

Mrs. Anglin was talking with her preschoolers. Rachel said she was going to be Tiger Lily when she grows up. Caitlin told Rachel she can't be Tiger Lily because Tiger Lily is a cartoon.

Then Rachel turned to Mrs. Anglin and asked, "Well, what are YOU going to be when YOU grow up?"

Chapter Sixteen

Angela, 5, takes ballet lessons. One week the teacher missed a lesson, so the next week she announced to her students that there would be a make-up lesson.

Angela ran to her teacher and hugged her with joy. "You mean we get to wear make-up?!" she exclaimed.

Paul, 5, was helping his father rake leaves.
"Dad, will you pay me?" Paul asked.
"Maybe, if you're a big help," Terry said.
"How about a dollar?" Paul asked.
"Maybe half a dollar," Terry replied.
"You going to tear it up?" Paul asked.

After she returned home from shopping, Vi told Chuck, 4, how hard she had looked for the Kool-Aid in the store. "I had to go up and down the aisles," she said.
"You mean there are hills in there?" Chuck asked.

Krista, 4, was watching her older sisters playing softball. She heard the girls shout "flyball" over and over.
After a few minutes, she asked, "Mom, just how does a ball fly?"

Karl, 6, took a break from playing to kneel down and tie his shoes.
Then an idea hit him. "Horses can't tie their shoes, can they?" he asked his mom.

Trent, 7, stubbed his toe and after a few weeks he began losing his toenail.
When he finally finished pulling off the toenail, he asked his father very seriously, "If I put this under my pillow, will I get any money?"

Jayden, 6, was looking at his open mouth in the mirror.
"What's that thing hanging in the back of my throat that looks like a punching bag?" he asked.

Sandy was babysitting for her niece Elizabeth, 6, on the day President Bill Clinton was inaugurated. The band started playing "The Star Spangled Banner."
"That's kind of an old song, isn't it?" Elizabeth asked.

Jeremy, 2, got his hair cut. His father complimented him on how nice his new haircut looked and asked him where he got his hair cut.
Jeremy looked puzzled and replied, "Right here on my head!"

Funny Kids

When the Woodwards put Sara and Jill to bed, they allow the sisters to talk for 10 minutes. Then they come back and tell them it is time to go to sleep.

One night they forgot to go back 10 minutes later. A few hours later Sara came out of the room, practically sleepwalking, and asked, "Can we go to sleep now?!"

Jeff, 3, was running around the house and driving Vi crazy. "Why don't you go outside and burn off some energy," she said.

Jeff looked at her, his eyes wide with amazement, "Can I have MATCHES?!" he asked.

Mr. Buffenbarger was visiting friends when their little girl jumped on his lap.

"Mary Lou!" the little girl's mother scolded. "He doesn't like to hold little girls like you!"

Mary Lou quickly got off Mr. Buffenbarger's lap. As she walked away she asked Mr. Buffenbarger, "You like to hold big girls like Mama?!"

Many years ago when Mrs. Bolton was teaching kindergarten, she held her students spellbound with her vivid and detailed description of the Pilgrims and the first Thanksgiving.

After the story the class was very quiet. Then a little boy looked up at her with big soulful eyes and asked, "Mrs. Bolton, was you there?!"

Marlies was chauffering her granddaughter Elizabeth, 7, and her great-granddaughter Kaitlyn, 6, to and from the Old Wayne Center One-Room Schoolhouse summer program.

One day for show-and-tell the girls took an old iron that had to be heated on a cook stove.

On the way Marlies explained to the girls how the iron was used. She told them that when the iron began to cool, you had to set it back on the cook stove and wait for it to get hot again. She told the girls that it was a job that took a long time.

When Marlies paused, Kaitlyn looked up at her and asked, "Why didn't you just put them in the microwave? You could've got done a lot faster!"

Chapter Seventeen

When Mum's the Word For An Aspiring Singer

It's hard to resist the temptation to think that your child can't master something just because you never could — or conversely to think that something will come easily for your child because it came easily to you.

It took great effort to keep a straight face. "You want to what?" I asked.

"I want to sing at the Fine Arts Festival," our 8-year-old repeated.

Elizabeth is a second-grader who since nursery school has wanted to be an actress. Her idol is Julie Andrews. Unfortunately, Elizabeth carries my genes for singing. She was born 90 years too late. She would have been a great star of the silent screen.

As a child I — like Elizabeth — sang with gusto. But after my family repeatedly requested, "Gracie, please don't sing!" I realized no one enjoyed the sounds but me. So I sang in my head or hummed very softly.

In music class I became good at moving my lips and not issuing a sound.

As I grew older, my singing didn't improve. I had songs inside of me that were dying to come out, but they couldn't. I felt handicapped.

I still avoid Christmas caroling unless there are at least half a dozen in the group. I never start the "Happy Birthday" song. At sporting events, after "Oh! say can you" I give up on our national anthem. There'd be "bombs bursting in air" if I ever hit the rest of the notes.

When our children were infants, I didn't sing them to sleep for fear of causing nightmares.

My favorite position in church is in front of a deep baritone. There I sing loudly, secure in the knowledge that he is drowning me out.

"I want to sing at the Fine Arts Festival," Elizabeth said for the third time.

"Why?" I asked.

"Because I want to be an actress."

"Well, I can't help you."

But I didn't want to crush her spirit. A little while later I was on the phone to my friend Cathie who sings like a lark.

"Could you teach her a song?" I asked.

Chapter Seventeen

"Can she sing?" Cathie asked. (My ears can't detect flats or sharps, but they detected doubt in Cathie's voice.)

"Well, that's just it," I said. "I don't think so ... Maybe you could teach her a really easy song that you just sort of talk through." (I had in mind something like Nancy Sinatra's "These Boots Are Made For Walking" but on a different subject. I didn't want my 8-year-old to sound like a heel!)

Cathie said Elizabeth should practice singing "Happy Birthday." Then Cathie would determine if Elizabeth would be able to sing a song for the festival or if she should do something else, like reciting a poem.

"Just don't sing it like Marilyn Monroe sang it to John F. Kennedy," father said when he heard about Elizabeth's upcoming audition.

"How did she sing it?" Elizabeth asked.

Terry threw back his head, closed his eyes and shaped his mouth like an "O."

"Haaaaaaaappy Biiiiiiiiirthday toooo yoooooooooooooou..."

"Oh," Elizabeth said.

For two days we heard Elizabeth fervently sing Happy Birthday to "dear Cathieeeeeeee." Sometimes she sang high. Sometimes low.

Each time she began, the 2-year-old came running to me yelling, "Cake! Cake!" I don't know which was harder — listening to Elizabeth or explaining to Paul that there was no cake.

After two days I suggested to Elizabeth that reciting a poem —maybe a poem that we would make up — might be more fun than singing at the festival.

"OK," she said, relieved that she didn't have to sing the Happy Birthday song any more.

The Fine Arts Festival is more than two months away. I'm not sure what we'll come up with.

Elizabeth still sings and dreams of being an actress. She doesn't seem to notice or care that she can't carry a tune.

And I bite my tongue to keep from making any comments.

(Jan. 23, 1990)

Chapter Eighteen
Potpourri

Potpourri is a mixture of flowers, herbs and spices that looks pretty, smells wonderful and adds a special touch to our homes. That's what this chapter is — a blending of stories to make a special chapter.

Gretchen was watching television with her son Aaron, 4. A commercial came on with a picture of Mount Rushmore.

After the commercial was over, Aaron asked, "Mom, are those men really fossilized?"

On a hot summer day Cheryl was bike riding with her three daughters, Brooke, 13, Autumn, 7, and Ginger, 3. When they started going up a steep hill, Cheryl, who had Ginger riding on the back of her bike, said, "Oh, Ginger, I don't think Mommy's going to make it up this hill."

Then Cheryl felt Ginger's small hands pressing hard against her back.

"I pusha you, Mommy. I pusha you, Mommy!" she said.

Ashley, 7, was talking about how ornery her 2-year-old brother Ian is.

Uncle Jack asked if Ian acted more like her dad or more like her mom.

Ashley thought for a few seconds and then said, "Actually, he acts like my dog!"

Tami was 3 when her grandmother told her to come in because it was getting dark and the mosquitoes were coming out.

"Grandma, come look!" Tami exclaimed. "The mosquitoes turned their lights on!" She was looking at lightning bugs.

A school counselor, Mrs. Farmer allows children to sign up to have lunch with her. One day Elizabeth and her third-grade friends were eating with Mrs. Farmer.

"Boy, Mrs. Farmer, you have a lot of gray hair," Elizabeth said.

"Well, I am almost 48 years old," Mrs. Farmer replied.

"Forty-eight," Elizabeth said thoughtfully. "No offense, Mrs. Farmer. But your hair looks older than you do!"

Chapter Eighteen

Evelyn asked her grandson Jason, 7, how he liked having his mother work. "Well, I was tired of her," he said. "But now I miss her."

Dolly, 6, was helping Aunt Vi Sutton to make beds. Aunt Vi was holding a pillow in her teeth as she pulled the pillow case on.

With a gleam in her eye, Dolly said, "Oh, Aunt Vi, what a big front tooth you have!"

I overheard Dustin, 6, and Lucy, 11, talking about photography. Lucy said a man she knows keeps his film in the refrigerator because it lasts longer that way. She added that the man takes lots of pictures when he goes on vacation.

"Does he take his refrigerator with him?" Dustin asked.

Rainelle and her son John, 9, were watching television. A commercial came on and stated, "If you have kids, you have germs!"

John turned to Rainelle and said, "I find that insulting."

On the evening news the Ogle family saw President Bush speaking at West Point Academy. The next morning they saw Bush on the morning news. It was a rebroadcast of his speech at West Point the day before.

As he looked at the president in surprise, Andrew, 7, exclaimed, "He's still there!"

"Do you know how I got to be 4?" Brad asked Mrs. Griebel. "I went to Chuck E Cheese's."

Zane told his Aunt Dawn that his parents were planting trees. "What kind of trees?" Dawn asked.

"Well, wood trees, of course!" he said.

Tomas Feininger, a geologist, used to have to fly from Quebec City to Ecuador. The least expensive way was to fly first to Florida.

As one of the trips approached Anna, 5, asked, "Daddy, why are we going to your ami?"

"Your ami?" asked a perplexed Tomas.

"Yes," Anna replied, "you're always talking about us going to Miami!"

Funny Kids

When Mrs. Shumaker picked Jason up from kindergarten, a little boy kept calling Jason's name.

"Do you know that little boy?" Mrs. Shumaker asked.

"I ought to," Jason said. "He gave me the hiccups yesterday!"

John, 3, told his mother Elizabeth she was driving too fast.

Elizabeth told him she was under the speed limit and doing just fine.

John, who was convinced his mother was speeding, hung his head. "I'm sad, I'm angry and I'm disappointed in you!" he said.

When Kerry turned 40 she received many gag gifts and balloons that spoke of being over the hill.

A few days after the big celebration, Dana, 7, gave her mother a lovely card she had made at school during recess. It said "Happy Birthday Mom" on the outside. On the inside was a drawing of a large black mound. It read, "40 - Over the Mountain!"

During a dry period, Lacey, 6, was at the home of her grandmother, Mrs. Nichols. Looking out the window at her parched lawn, Mrs. Nichols said, "My grass is really dying."

"You better call 911!" Lacey exclaimed.

When waitresses at Richard's Restaurant asked Kyrie' how old she was, she said, "I'm STILL 3!" as if it had been SUCH a long time!

Blake, 4, was in his grandmother's paneled sunroom.

"I don't like this room," he said, referring to the paneling. "I prefer rooms that have skin (wallpaper)!"

Mrs. Liedel sprained her ankle. It swelled quite large and stretched her sock. Derek, 6, who says he wants to be a doctor, examined Mrs. Liedel to see what the problem was.

His medical pronouncement: "One sock is bigger than the other."

Jonathan, 4, was outside with his mother Terrie. He looked up at the moon and said with surprise, "Mom, the moon broke apart!"

Then after a moment of thought, he said, "No, it's not broken. It is just hiding in the dark."

Chapter Eighteen

Karen, 4, was enjoying a bag of jelly beans when the family went through a drive-through carwash. It was Karen's first time. When the jets came on, she said, "My jelly beans are scared!"

Jarod, 3, was looking out the window.
"Look, Jarod, it's spitting snow," his mother Susan said.
"It's spitting snow?" Jarod asked. With excitement he went to his brother Nicolas, 6, and said, "Did you know snow could spit?"

Cindy's little girl was watching closely as the hairdresser applied a reddish product to her mother's hair.
"Is that Arby sauce in your hair?" she asked her mother.

A little boy said that whenever he needs money he knows where to find it... under his father's chair.

Brooke, 3: Me want more milk.
Nammy (a former teacher): I want more milk.
Brooke: No, ME want more milk!

Terry had driven for many hours. As it got darker, he started to yawn.
Paul, 7, called from the back seat, "You can have my pillow, Dad!"

Phillip, 3, said his brother's name was going to be Nicholas. "Mommy and Daddy can call him Nicholas," he said. "But I get to call him Nickel."

Suffering from a case of hiccups, preschooler Zachary asked his teacher, "Am I going to blow up?"

At circle time Mrs. Grubb asked the children what their full names were. When it was her turn, Anna looked at Mrs. Grubb with a puzzled face and said, "I give up!"

On the first day of preschool every child had a nametag. After about an hour Cassy asked, "Teacher, can I take my pricetag off?"

Nathan, 5, went to the doctor because he had a cold. Later he told his Aunt Stephanie, "Don't get close to me or you'll get what I've got."
"What's that?" Stephanie asked.
"Medication," Nathan replied.

Funny Kids

Wyllie used to sit for hours working on the computer. Little Jake found a small pillow with letters stenciled on it and put it on the seat of the rocker in the living room. He sat on the ottoman and "typed" on the pillow. Every once in a while he would lean WAY back, gazing intently at the back of the rocker, then continue to "type." Sue asked him why he had to lean so far back to see his "screen."

"Well, that's how Uncle Wyllie does it," Jake said.

Uncle Wyllie wears bifocals.

Dex, 3, was intent on watching his Uncle Gary, an Indiana State Police officer, prepare for work.

As Gary strapped on his gun belt and adjusted his hat, Dex followed by strapping on his toy gun and strategically placing his wide-brimmed hat on his own head.

Dex looked up, eyeballing his uncle's gun and solemnly asked, "You got batteries in yours?"

Chapter Nineteen

The First Day of School

"There is no frigate like a book to take us lands away."
Emily Dickinson

Summer's wayward curls had been shorn. The new back pack, with new pencils, erasers, watercolors, glue and scissors, was slung over the knob on the front door.

The new bedtime, one hour earlier than usual, had been carefully adhered to for a week.

"She is so excited," the mother told the first-grade teacher at a chance meeting a few days before the first day of school. "She talks about school all the time. We've been working on her words.

"She can't wait to see her kindergarten friends again and be in school the whole day. And take her lunch. And walk home with her friends.

"She's so full of anticipation. She knows pretty soon she'll be able to read whole books and write sentences and stories. It's a real turning point in her life. Almost like adolescence ... like beginning college or getting her first job.

"In fact," and the mother paused reflectively, "I've noticed she's been a little edgy the past few days. Almost like she's scared. It's on her mind all the time.

"I think first grade would be the best grade to teach," the mother rushed on, only slightly conscious of the teacher's understanding smile. "The children are so ready to learn ... so full of enthusiasm.

"It's almost like the Helen Keller story. Every day would seem like an adventure. Whole new worlds open up. There's no other grade that would offer such rewards... The children are SO eager, SO excited. It's such a milestone."

"Yes," the experienced teacher observed. "First grade is exciting for the students."

Then she paused and smiled at the mother, so full of anticipation. "But I think first grade is even more exciting for the parents."

(First published on Aug. 27, 1985, this essay is dedicated to Kay Howard who was the first-grade teacher for all four of my children.)

Chapter Twenty

Two Boys and A Picture

"O Lord, thou art our father; we are the clay, and thou our potter; and we all are the work of thy hand."

Isaiah 64:8

My 7-year-old was watching TV when I interrupted to show him the picture.

"Who is this?" I asked, thrusting a photograph of a brown-haired little boy in front of his face.

Paul studied the picture.

"Who is it?" I asked again.

"Me?" he said hesitantly.

The boy in the picture looked exactly like Paul. But he was wearing an old-fashioned dress shirt with a pouffy black tie — a getup Paul has never worn.

"Yes, it's you," I said.

Paul looked again closely. "Really?" he asked.

We like to tease in our family, so I said, "Yes, it's you. Don't you remember?"

But one of his sisters had seen the picture. "It's not you, Paul," she said. "It's Mohler!"

Mohler was my father's father. He died 13 years ago. But it seems like yesterday.

His full name was George Mohler Studebaker Witwer. (He was an only son, so I guess that's why his parents piled so many names on him.) But everyone, even we grandkids, knew him as Mohler.

Mohler S. Witwer
1902-1981

Mohler was born late in his parents' life. His only sibling was a sister who was much older. A beautiful redhead, she died in a tragic riding accident when she was in her 20s. Mohler's doting parents spoiled him as a child. In later years one of his favorite possessions was a large imitation gold paperweight that said, "MINE!"

The challenges of the Depression helped to change Mohler from a pampered youth into a serious, hard-working man. He worked long hours, made difficult decisions and took risks. After stressful years, he came out well.

Chapter Twenty

I probably saw the photograph many years ago, but I didn't pay any attention to it until now — now that my son looks exactly like the picture. The picture seemed to leap out at me a few weeks ago when I spotted it on a visit to Gaga's house.

I made a copy of the old photograph, and I catch myself looking at it often, remembering Mohler and comparing him to Paul.

Mohler had a wonderful sense of humor and was always ready to play a practical joke. I see the beginnings of that in Paul.

Mohler was a reader and very curious. He loved cars, boats, photography, golf, cribbage, taking trips, collecting things and telling stories.

Mohler told his best family and business stories at the dinner table. He and Gaga (our name for his wife, our grandmother) enjoyed lengthy cocktail hours and long, leisurely meals in their stately dining room. I often didn't understand the conversations, but I liked hearing the grown-ups' voices and laughter.

So I look at the photograph and think about the way Mohler was as a grandfather and imagine him as a little boy. Now that I'm getting older, and see my exterior changing with time, I can think of my grandparents not just as senior citizens, but as kids, too. My mother's mother used to say she was a kid trapped in an old lady's body. Now I understand. Over the years your personality and interests basically stay the same. It's just your body that changes.

Sometimes when I watch Paul run down the sidewalk or drop down from a high branch in a tree, I think about Mohler and what he was like playing in his backyard in South Bend. Did he chase birds and catch bugs like Paul does? Did he get into sweets and then, when his mother discovered the cookies or brownies had vanished, innocently say, "It was an accident."

Did he do cartwheels and handstands in the living room?

I've often wished I could have known my grandparents when they were my age. We would have been good friends.

Paul and Mohler would have been best friends. I can imagine the pranks they would have pulled and the hours they would have spent at cards. Paul loves all card games, and is beginning to master cribbage, Mohler's favorite game.

They would have enjoyed taking pictures together. Paul bought a camera with his birthday money, and he takes as many pictures as I (the person who pays for the film and the processing) will allow. Mohler had a darkroom in his basement. Paul would have been enthralled if Mohler could have shown him how film is developed. He would have loved the darkness, the smell of the chemicals and figuring out the best way to crop and print the pictures.

Sometimes children have little in common with their parents and grandparents — because of the different times they live in, changing family circumstances and the unpredictability of genes.

Funny Kids

Actually, Mohler would have argued that genes — at least his genes — are predictable. He claimed that everything good that we grandchildren did was because of his genes. He especially bragged about how his genes were responsible for my sister Vi's outstanding success in college and law school. One Christmas Vi gave him a pair of Levi jeans — to replace the genes he had given her! Mohler thought the jeans joke was great, and he laughed about it for years.

Mohler knew we were unique individuals. But he liked to talk about his influence.

Parents need to remember that each child is unique and should be allowed to pursue his or her own goals and interests. Children should be taught that their gifts are from God, not from an ancestor.

But sometimes we get a child who looks or acts "just like" a certain relative. And it's fun to compare.

(Sept. 20, 1994)

Chapter Twenty-One

To Grandparents' House We Go!

We often hear the phrase, "Stop and smell the roses." If there are grandchildren around, the phrase could be interpreted to mean, "Stop and hug the grandchildren!" The time spent with grandchildren has long-lasting rewards for all the "grands" — parents and children.

"Boy, that's old!" Joel, 4, said when he learned the age of a great-aunt who was celebrating her 80th birthday.

His grandmother explained to him that the Bible says if you obey your parents, you'll live a long life.

Without hesitating, Joel replied, "You can expect me to die any minute!"

Margie saw her grandmother take out her upper plate, and asked, "Are you going to take your eyes out now?"

Ron, 5, asked his grandma if she had toy cars to play with when she was little.

"Yes," she said. "But they weren't plastic like the one you have. I had a rubber one, an Auburn Cord."

Thoughtfully Ron fingered his small car. Then he handed it to his grandma as if bestowing a great treasure.

"Here," he said. "You may play with this when you want to. Maybe it will help replace your lost childhood."

Linda had her grandson Colton, 22 months, in the back seat. He was running the automatic window up and down. It was beginning to get cool in the car, so Linda held the window closed from the front seat.

"Grandma, needs new battery!" Colton said from the back seat.

Chapter Twenty-One

Kara, 8, came to her grandma's after school and found her painting a picture. After watching for a while she stated, "Grandma, you're pretty good."

Teasing, grandma said, "Oh, yes, I'm really good!"

Looking thoroughly disgusted, Kara said, "Oh, Grandma, stop complicating yourself!"

At a family gathering Dustin, 3, was spinning around. He lost his balance and hit his head on a shelf, causing a deep wound. His parents Fred and Cathie had to rush him to the emergency room where he received stitches.

A few days later Dustin's grandmother, Julie Atz, came up with a system that she thought would prevent future accidents.

"Remember what ATZ stands for," she told Fred and Cathie. "A stands for Anticipate danger. T stands for Try to intercept. Z stands for Zero in on the child."

Fred, while he appreciated his mother-in-law's concern, told her past history indicates that ATZ stands for: A - Anticipate danger. T - Try to intercept. Z - Zip the child to the hospital!"

Sarah pointed out a big spider to her Grandmother Nissen.
"How many legs do spiders have?" Sarah asked.
"Lots of them. Eight."
"Grandma, how come you never see a spider with its babies?"
"I don't know, Sarah. But you are right. I have never seen a spider with its babies like you do a duck or a raccoon."
"I bet I know why, Grandma," Sarah said. "It's because the spider mom doesn't want to take the time to tie all those shoes!"

Jessica, 4, was playing at her grandparents' farm when she found a ticket near the barn. Taking it to the house, she excitedly told her grandpa, "The cow lost her pricetag!"

Courtney's grandpa was teasing her, and she was ignoring him.
"You don't love me, do you?" he asked.
"Yes, I love you," Courtney replied. "But I love your grandma better!"

Nicolas said, "I have a dad whose name is Mark. He has a dad. His name is Grandpa."

Funny Kids

Jean and her granddaughter Elizabeth, 5, made some homemade goodies for Myrtle Black, who was celebrating her 103rd birthday.

Jean wanted to impress on her granddaughter how old Mrs. Black was. "Do you know how much 103 is?" she asked Elizabeth.

"Well, I know what 101 dalmations are!" Elizabeth said.

Tara, 5, was uncomfortable with a bad head cold and couldn't sleep.
"Grandma, will you count sheep for me?" she asked.

A grandmother's ex-husband had a new girlfriend. After her grandson met the new girlfriend, he told his grandma, "She's not as fat as you, Grandma, but you're prettier!"

Neal used the phone at his sister's house. The smell of his aftershave lingered on the receiver.

A little while later his sister's grandson, Dustin, 8, answered the phone. It was a man who wanted to talk to his grandfather, who wasn't home at the time.

"Wow, that guy had on strong aftershave lotion," Dustin told his grandmother. "I could smell it clear through the phone!"

A little girl encountered her grandmother putting on her bra. The grandmother was hooking it in front.

"No, no, Grandma, you're not doing it right," the little girl said.

"I'm not?" the grandma said with surprise.

"No, Grandma, you're not doing it right," the girl repeated. "You are supposed to turn it around and put your bombs in first!"

Jeryl was volunteering at school, helping first-graders to put stories into their computers. One boy started his story this way: "My grandpa mows. My grandpa rakes."

Then there was total silence. Jeryl asked the boy if he could think of anything else his grandpa did. He looked at Jeryl and said very emphatically, "Well, you know, he really doesn't do anything. My grandma does all the work. Can I start over and tell my story about her?"

Ron heard Grandma Balzer playing the piano and singing. He brought a radio to her and asked, "Do you care if I change the station?"

Jeff, 12, told his grandparents about an elderly man who was "all mixed up and confused — he must have that 'old-timer's disease.'" He meant Alzheimer's.

Chapter Twenty-One

Seeing that there was no car in the grandparents' driveway, Julia said, "It doesn't look like they're home."

"Oh, they're home," Samuel said with certainty.

"How do you know?" Julia asked with surprise.

"Because they are retired," Samuel said.

Chase, 7, told his mother Tammy that "Grandma Herron is my great-great grandmother."

"No, she's just your great-grandmother," Tammy said.

"Well, anyway, Mom, she's still pretty terrific!" Chase said.

A 4-year-old asked his great-grandmother how old she was.

"Eighty-two," she replied.

He looked at her with wide eyes and asked, "Did you start at one?"

Following a big holiday meal, people started yawning and dozing off.

Observing how relaxed everyone was, Donnie, 10, said, "I think grandma sprays tired stuff in the air."

Breeana told her grandmother that she could read all the books in the library, but she just couldn't figure out the words!

On Grandparents' Day at St. John Lutheran School, Sophia's grandma couldn't make it, so Carol, the school secretary, stood in for her.

Later when Carol came in the first-grade room to leave a message, Sophia called out with excitement: "Hey, she's my fake grandma!"

Maxine, the great-grandmother of Cort, 8, said, "I don't think Kara (Cort's little sister) likes to come to our house as much as you do."

"Well, she isn't into old people," Cort said.

"Oh, and you are?" Maxine asked.

"Grandmas and grandpas, I am!" Cort replied.

Bambi, 6, and her grandfather, Gabby, were practicing golf. They were close to Gabby's car and could hear a tape Gabby was playing.

"What's that music?" Bambi asked.

"That's Glenn Miller's 'In the Mood,'" Gabby said. "It's music your grandma and I used to dance to. Do you like it?"

"Yes," Bambi said, moving in time with the beat. "But I can't stand still to hit a ball!"

Funny Kids

Kara was sitting on her grandpa's lap and messing up his hair.

"Honey, don't mess my hair up," he said.

"Grandpa, I want to see how you look when you get up in the morning!" Kara said.

Lowell and Loretta took their granddaughter, Tara, 6, to the movie. They got there early and had time to kill

"Let's go window shopping," Loretta said.

"Grandma!" Tara scolded. "You don't need new windows!"

Nick, 20 months, was at his grandmother's house. He went in the bathroom, where his grandmother had just gotten out of the shower and was drying herself.

Pointing to his grandmother's backside, he said excitedly, "Basketball! Basketball!"

"Grandpa, are you old?" Lauren asked.

"I guess I am," he replied.

"Is Grandma old, too?"

"Yes, she's old, too."

There was a long pause, and Lauren said, "I wish you and Grandma were both NEW again."

The Osterlunds were picking blueberries.

"Mom, I know how these berries are like people," Alicia, 6, said.

"Oh, how?" Mrs. Osterlund asked.

"When they are greenish-white they are babies. They are teen-agers when they are red. When they are blue, they are grown-ups. And they are grandparents when they are in the pie."

Do you think she considers a grandparent's role to be delicious?

Chapter Twenty-Two

Little Elves (Kids and Christmas)

The best Christmases are the ones that include children. Listen to their Christmas lists, their questions and their observations. The holidays are a magical time when anything can happen — and usually does.

When Jamie was 3, her parents, Hal and Cheryl, wanted to make a true believer in Santa out of her. Her parents had a good idea that Santa was going to get her a stove, refrigerator and sink set, so every time Jamie saw Santa, her parents told her to ask for a stove, refrigerator and sink.

When Jamie got home from her grandparents' house on Christmas Eve, Santa Claus had been there. When Jamie saw that Santa had brought her the kitchen set that she had been asking for, she turned to Cheryl and said, "See, Mom, you can be naughty and still get what you want!"

Dana, 4, was finally brave enough to sit on Santa's lap. At a local store she met Santa. He asked her what her name was, how old she was and the other questions that Santa usually asks.

A few weeks later she told her mother Kerry, "I thought you said Santa knew everything about me."

"Oh, he does," Kerry assured her.

"Then why did he have to ask me what my name was?" Dana asked.

Three-year-old Brittni Nicole was learning Bible songs including "Sing Hosanna."

Her Grandma Ruth asked Brittni to sing "Sing Hosanna."

"No, Grandma, it's not 'Sing Hosanna,'" Brittni said. "It's 'Sing for Santa.'"

Grandpa and Grandma Croy were taking Andrew, 4, to Wolcottville. As they passed St. Gasper's Church, Andrew reported that he had been there at Christmas to see Uncle Bill when he was in a play.

"That's when he was that wise guy!" Andrew said. (He meant Wise Man!)

Chapter Twenty-Two

Ruth and Paul, who are foster parents, make a big deal out of Santa Claus because some of their foster children have never had Christmas before.

A few weeks before Christmas a 4-year-old was being naughty.

"Don't you want Santa to come to see you?" Ruth asked.

"Yes," the 4-year-old said. "But if he doesn't, we can take the presents out of the closet and put them under the tree ourselves."

Our four children received Advent calendars that had pieces of chocolate inside. They enjoyed opening the little doors each morning and starting off the day with a bit of chocolate.

A few days before Christmas, Catherine, 6, was asked to list what she wanted for Christmas. Her list concluded, "And a January Advent calendar!"

On a cold winter day Linda saw a 4-year-old boy with bare feet inside his shoes.

"Where are your stockings?" she asked.

"Mom put them away right after Christmas," he replied.

At a family gathering, Kathy suggested that family members exchange children's names for Christmas. Later that evening Brittany said, "Did we 'change names for Christmas?"

"Oh, we forgot," Kathy said. "We'll do it later.

"Well, what's Andrew's name going to be?" Brittany asked.

Joe, 10, was very impatient about getting the family's Christmas tree. Although it was several weeks before Christmas, the neighbors had their tree up, and Joe wanted his family to have their tree up, too.

One Sunday morning he faked being sick so that he could stay home from church. His father was supposed to be watching him, but he forgot Joe was there. After his mother was gone, Joe got his bicycle and wagon and went to the neighbors with a saw. When his mother got home, she saw a trail of pine needles. When she went in, she saw an 8-foot Christmas tree.

Joe was in his bed. "Look what I found, Mom!" he said.

At Christmas when the Spriggs family gathered for Christmas dinner, Nicolas was watching his Grandma Ocie put the turkey on the serving platter.

Noticing the skin on the turkey, Nicolas said, "Grandma, you forgot to take his pantyhose off!"

Funny Kids

Matthew, 8, told his mother he wanted a remote control car for Christmas.

"Those are very expensive," Sandy said.

"Well, let Santa bring it," Matthew said.

A few days later Sandy told Matthew she had been Christmas shopping.

"You better keep the receipts in case Santa brings the same things," Matthew said.

My sister and her family drove from Maryland to spend Thanksgiving in Indiana. Soon after they arrived, my sister realized she had forgotten to bring the Christmas presents. She was extremely upset, because that meant she would have to mail them.

Paul, 5, was dismayed to see his aunt to upset. He tried to console her by saying, "Maybe Santa Claus will bring them here."

On a holiday car trip we were singing "The Twelve Days of Christmas." After we had sung for a while, I realized Catherine, 7, was not singing "and a partridge in a pear tree."

She was belting out, "and a portrait of a palm tree!"

A few days before Christmas, Carly, 4, emerged from her bedroom. With all the solemnity a child can muster, she announced that she was a good girl.

"Why are you a good girl?" her mother Eileen asked.

Carly told her she had cleaned her toy-strewn room.

"Why did you do that?" Eileen asked.

"Well," Carly said, "Santa has to have a way to get through here somehow!"

The fourth-graders at St. John Lutheran School were told to write stories about their Christmas memories. This is an excerpt from Dorothy Lee's story:

"My family woke up on Christmas Day. We opened our presents from Santa. My brother Jeff was so excited. Jeff was happy because he got Barney slippers. Chuck and Jeff both got puzzles. Lucy and I both got hair stuff and more. My dad got a whole lot of candy. My mom got nothing as usual."

Chapter Twenty-Two

When Jane put out the manger scene, she carefully told Carrie, 2, the Christmas story, so that she would be thinking about the real meaning of Christmas.

"Where does Jesus live?" Carrie asked.

Jane told her.

"What is his phone number?" Carrie asked.

Later Carrie told Jane, "When Jesus comes to visit, I want to give him cookies, Mommy."

Niccole, 4, was afraid of Santa. When she saw him greeting children in a store, she said to him, "I'm NOT sitting on your lap! If you give me your phone number, I'll call you when I have time!"

"I'm NOT sitting on your lap! If you give me
your phone number, I'll call you when I have time!"

Chapter Twenty-Three

A Homemaker Is Priceless

"A good wife ... is far more precious than jewels."
Proverbs 31:10

A life insurance salesman pointed out to my husband and me a magazine article entitled, "What's a homemaker worth?"

The article said statisticians have come up with an average value of $600 per week for the "myriad services" performed by a typical homemaker. That adds up to an annual salary of $31,200. If you add fringe benefits, the "grand compensation value" is $41,500 per year.

The salesman implied I should be pretty proud of my worth as a homemaker.

I didn't argue with him at the time. But I know my husband couldn't afford to hire someone to do all the things I do at home, and I think putting a dollar value on a homemaker's worth is silly.

The job titles (dietary consultant, labor mediator, consumer analyst, clinical psychologist, etc.) are pompous, and the salary figures are inflated.

For example, the article says that when a homemaker serves as a dietary consultant, she (most homemakers are female) should earn a minimum of $10 per hour, according to the U.S. Department of Labor.

What mother of young children can unblushingly claim to be a "dietary consultant?" I took home economics in seventh grade; I try to keep up on the nutritional content of our breakfast cereals, and I have a few cookbooks. But not one of my four children has ever consulted me about a diet plan. When I mention that it would be nice to take at least one bite of broccoli, they fall writhing to the floor and angrily remind me that they drank orange juice for breakfast so they got their vitamins.

I don't "consult" the children when I bypass the artificially colored, artificially flavored, sugar-coated cereals that cost more per pound than steak. And they don't consult me when they feed their broccoli to the dog.

I remind my husband to eat tuna two or three times a week to lower his cholesterol. And he does. But the dietary "consultation," which takes about 30 seconds a week, is worth less than 50 cents a week, figured on a $10 per hour basis. Even if

Chapter Twenty-Three

you add in my lectures when he goes for another dish of ice cream, my "dietary consulting" fees total less than $1 a week.

The article says when a homemaker dons a chauffeur's cap, her salary might increase to $12 an hour. (Does it make any difference if you got a D+ in driver's education and still refuse to drive in big city traffic and can't parallel park?)

As a math tutor, depending on where you live and the complexity of the calculations involved, a homemaker's expertise might garner $5 to $50 an hour, the article states. But I'm not sure I'm going to be able to make it through middle school math homework. Already my children sometimes come home from school and say, "Mom, you got it wrong!"

"If you're looking for some heart-to-heart counseling, such service is worth roughly $60 per hour in the clinical psychology open market. Or what about a plumber when the toilet overflows from a tennis ball lodged in its drain cavity? Try $36 just for showing up at the door."

I've never solved a plumbing problem without the help of my husband and/or the plumber. I've also never done electrical or carpentry work, two other tasks the article includes in its homemaker's list of duties. I change lightbulbs and hang pictures. But am I a flop because I'm not an electrician? Because I pay someone to do our taxes? Because I don't hang my own wallpaper?

I'm proud to be a wife and mother of four. I stay busy cooking, cleaning, washing, shopping, planning, organizing, driving, volunteering and writing. Much of my work, such as sorting socks and carpooling kids, is boring. At other times, homemaking is back-breaking, nerve-wracking or frustrating. I lament the fact that none of my dinners please more than 50 percent of the people I serve, my children seem to enter adolescence early and that an orderly house (not to mention an orderly life) is a pipe dream.

But I'm happy. I love my family and our small town lifestyle. I take time for reading and doing fun things with family and friends. I don't feel guilty when I take a nap.

The compensation I want for doing 12 loads of wash a week and mediating disputes that seem to verge on World War III is not someone telling me I'm worth $41,500 a year.

Besides, who would pay me?

I don't want grandiose titles like clinical psychologist or dietary consultant. My children will never, EVER ask me if they have exceeded their recommended allowance of dietary fats or would one more granola bar be OK?

As a chauffeur I don't doff my hat and transport my children at their bidding. They walk to and from school except in blinding rain or snow — and they're healthier for it. Many times if they demand to be taken someplace I say, "No, I'm not your chauffeur." (My other quotable quotes are: "I'm not your maid" and "I'm not your servant.")

The article says homemakers are also gardeners, snow shovelers, sports coaches and Sunday school teachers. I'm none of those. My husband is all of them — and I'm grateful.

I'm not Superwoman. I don't want to be. I don't want to be a grim, plunger-wielding martyr who works 24 hours a day.

I want to be a happy wife and mother. A happy mother is a prerequisite to a happy family.

I don't know what the dollar value of my services is. But I couldn't care less because I'll never be paid in dollars and cents.

The payment I want is love and respect and — is this too much to ask? — acceptance when I serve broccoli.

(July 5, 1988)

"A chicken that lays eggs is a ___ (hen). One boy wrote 'MOM.'"

"OK, Daddy. I ready go for ride!"

Our Family Stories

"This is the day which the Lord has made; we will rejoice and be glad in it."
                              Psalm 118:24

Our Family Stories

Our Family Stories

Our Family Stories

The children were told to cross their legs and sit like pretzels...
"But I like straight pretzels!"

"I didn't think I'd have anything like this until my WEDDING!"

Our Family Stories

Our Family Stories

Our Family Stories

Our Family Stories

Noah the cat is 98 in cat years. "Does Noah know he is an adult?"